Ancient Crosses of the
Three Choirs Counties

Ancient Crosses of the Three Choirs Counties

Marion Freeman

To Christine and David and their families, with all my love.

Back cover illustration:
The cross at Wyre Piddle by Ms M. Hutcheon of Kempsey, Worcesterhsire.

First published 2009

The History Press
The Mill, Brimscombe Port
Stroud, Gloucestershire, GL5 2QG
www.thehistorypress.co.uk

© Marion Freeman, 2009

The right of Marion Freeman to be identified as the Author
of this work has been asserted in accordance with the
Copyrights, Designs and Patents Act 1988.

British Library Cataloguing in Publication Data.
A catalogue record for this book is available from the British Library.

ISBN 978 0 7524 5288 3

Typesetting and origination by The History Press
Printed in Great Britain

Contents

Acknowledgements

First and foremost to my long-suffering husband who refuses to share the title name but without whom this book would never have reached fruition. He has driven many miles throughout the Three Counties during the past few years in our search to find as many countryside crosses as possible. He has also been responsible for the map references which are included in the book. Without his support and encouragement I would probably have given up!

My thanks are also due to the following: Laurie Clifton Crick (Wick), Raymond Honey (Bosbury), and the late Bob Cross (Sevenstoke), for so generously sharing with me the information gained by them in their researches. Thanks also to Jane Birdsall (Snowshill Manor), Rex Lofts (Woolstone), and Dr J. Barnes of Ashelworth. The staff at the Gloucestershire Archives and Tourist Information Centres at Ross, Cirencester, Dursley and Ledbury have also been of great assistance, not forgetting Glenda and Sharon at my local TIC. Also my grateful thanks must go to those vicars and churchwardens through-out the Three Counties who have considerately replied to my letters, not least those at Pauntley and Iron Acton, and I must also make mention of the many church guides from which I have been able to glean information.

Preface

No doubt everyone has their own perception of a typical English village. These would probably be of a place where the past is always present, and where community life is of prime importance. As to the scene, this could well include a church, and maybe an additional chapel, at least one pub, and a variety of houses built from a selection of materials. On its outskirts are farmhouses and outbuildings. There would usually be a nearby river forded by bridges of varying types and ages, and maybe an old manor house; perhaps a castle, and in most cases a village hall, the latter even more so during recent times when grants from the Millennium Lottery Fund have allowed failing halls to be renovated and new, enlarged community centres to be constructed. Other additions to the village scene might well be a pump on a village green, a well or an ancient churchyard cross.

Having been fascinated by all these things that epitomise the British countryside and its many facets since childhood, I have long been interested in bee boles and bridges, cairns and canals, maypoles and markets – the list is endless and a never-ending source of research and investigation. Chief among these for me are the many countryside and churchyard crosses that can be discovered throughout the land. Built in a variety of styles and consisting of a selection of materials, they stand (in spite of orders from Oliver Cromwell during the Commonwealth period to destroy them) in differing stages of preservation, an historical and nostalgic throwback to the past.

Since childhood I've been a collector of Arthur Mee's books, published in the King's England series, and for many years have used these as a guide when visiting various places throughout the country. In many cases, he mentions in passing that there are remains of crosses to be found in churchyards. However, my interest in the subject was aroused even further when, some thirty years ago, I borrowed from the library a book by Alfred Rimmer entitled *Ancient Stone Crosses of England*. Published in 1875, it surveyed many of their sites, mentioning their historical and religious importance. Having already visited some of these I found it fascinating to note differences that had occurred during the intervening years, which changes have, of course, altered even further since then.

For the purpose of this book I am mainly concentrating on those crosses found in the past and those still present in Gloucestershire, Herefordshire and Worcestershire – Three Counties recognised more or less as an entity since the advent of the Three Counties Musical Festival, of which Sir Edward Elgar later became such a champion.

This prestigious musical festival takes place annually and successively in each of the Three Counties. The latter contains my beautiful hometown of Pershore, a name deriving from the Anglo Saxon word meaning a slope or bank where osiers grow. Although it had long been pretty certain there was a Saxon settlement in the area, it was not until renovation work was carried out on the abbey here in 1994 that proof, in the form of old Saxon foundations, was revealed.

In medieval times it is thought there were four crosses in the town; the high cross situated at the end of Broad Street, Boyer's Cross at the top end of the High Street, Newlands Cross (site unknown) and Hampton Cross, probably near the bridge. Thus there would have been one in the centre of town and one at each of the main road entrances. Although the remnant of the cross now standing in the abbey grounds lost its original tabernacle top long ago, this is identical to a description given by an old inhabitant in 1865, and is said to have been moved from Wyre Piddle to the Abbey House grounds in 1844. The base of the older cross was incorporated in a new one following the First World War but this was subsequently badly damaged by a severe gale and probably moved, minus the modern head-cross, to its present position nearer the abbey building following the demolition of Abbey House during the 1930s. It now stands on two steps topped by a solid broached base or socket-stone and the modern shaft.

Having such an example on my own doorstep so to speak, I guess it's not that unusual I should take a special interest in the origins and histories of such erections. I owe a huge debt to my husband, who has driven me hundreds of miles through the countryside as we endeavour to discover interesting, historic and unusual reminders of the past, and we must, during the past few years, have visited well over 500 churchyards in the Three

Pershore Cross as it appeared in the early 1900s.

Pershore Cross as it is today.

Counties. It is probably inevitable that we may have missed some that still retain these ancient remains, and if I've omitted to include any particularly dear to you, I apologise and would be extremely grateful to hear from you. Likewise, whilst I have attempted to be completely accurate, it could well be that in trying to cover such a large area, errors may have occurred. Naturally my information has been gleaned from many sources and I cannot guarantee these themselves are 100 per cent accurate, or that our interpretations are wholly correct. If any reader is able to correct, or add to, the information I would also be very pleased to hear of this. In this way does historical research expand and improve.

There does seem to be a dearth of information about these crosses and on many occasions, even where churches have a written guide, there is no mention of a cross that may stand by their building. Others contain only a fleeting reference. Unfortunately, in recent times more and more churches are finding it necessary to keep their buildings closed and we've been disappointed to be unable to visit several, even though we confine our visits mainly to Sundays. It was especially upsetting to find some churches closed even on Easter Sunday.

Occasionally local historians have undertaken more detailed research into those crosses in their vicinity and their findings may have been lodged with local Record Offices. But on the whole it has been very difficult to trace any detailed history. The majority of books written about the crosses were compiled some years ago and can be very out of date, although they contain invaluable information as to those in existence some 150 years earlier, and they usually show drawings of the remains as they appeared then. They are certainly much more detailed than this book attempts to be. In addition, later renovations and rebuilding have often resulted in the discovery of odd heads, shafts or sockets hidden away for safety or just forgotten, overgrown, or used for other purposes. Thankfully where such remains are rediscovered they are usually being carefully restored.

Therefore every visit we undertake is something of an adventure – what shall we find?

I

Early Times

Britain in early times was a wild, uncivilised country covered with dense forests stretching for many miles. These lands were intersected by bare rocky wastes, wide fens and sinking marshlands with dwellings occurring only on the uplands – such places as the Downs, the Cotswolds and Chilterns and the vast plain at Salisbury. Here travellers from Gaul would trade with the Britons of the west and south-west dealing in tin, lead and copper, those early inhabitants gradually learning of life outside their islands. They themselves were known to be brave and fearless fighters who carried spears, swords and shields and used heavy war chariots, their hill camps fortified by stakes. In contrast the Britons of the wilder parts of the north and west were relatively untouched by the newcomers, living their old ways and still relying mainly on hunting and fishing.

Even in the towns there would be little in the way of substantial building, with probably the earliest being houses of worship, first in wood, later replaced by stone. Homes of the ordinary people would certainly be of wood, based on a framework of beams sunk into the ground and fastened by wooden pegs. This framework could be covered in planks but was more likely to be of wattle and daub – an outline consisting of willow or hazel and covered by a mixture of clay, straw and cow dung, with floors of beaten earth. Roofs would be thatched with straw or reeds whilst windows were just small gaps cut into the walls, which could be covered with wattle shutters.

The country was still split into numerous tribes who were sharply divided and kept strictly to their own ways. However there was one aspect in which they were united – that of the Druid religion. Little is really known of their rites or of their order of worship, although they are thought to have worshipped some form of nature, holding the oak tree in great reverence with mistletoe, often growing from its branches, being a very sacred emblem. Since it was such a secret religion, much of their hold over people could well have been though a sense of fear. Thus it was that when Julius Caesar landed at Pevensey in 55 BC he found the rule of the Druids to be a very powerful and cohesive strength. His foray into the country was short-lived and although he invaded again the following year he was only able to make a very partial conquest. It was nearly ninety years before any further hostile invaders attempted to return to Britain.

The Romans, tempted by the vast wealth known to be available in Britain, were soon considering more attacks and in AD 43 Aulus Plautius launched a fierce attack against the south and south-east, gaining a tenuous foothold in the country. Struggles between the Romans and four British tribes who had banded together under Caratacus continued for five years until, in AD 50, Ostorius Scapula overthrew Caratacus thus gaining a real hold over part of the land. When he was overthrown, Caratacus was delivered to Rome where he was regarded as a great catch and paraded in triumph. He became so famous that following a speech before the Emperor Claudius he and his family were granted a free pardon.

During the next few years, lands to the north and west of Britain were gradually conquered, and in AD 61 Suetonius Paulinus decided on a final foray into Wales. Crossing the Menai Straights to Anglesey, the Druid's Holy Isle, he was able to rout and remove them, cutting down their groves and burning their oak trees. However, whilst he was thus occupied in the west, the Icenei tribe, under Boadicea, was able to invade Colchester, burning the city and killing the inhabitants of the garrison. Her revolt spread, with not only Romans being killed but any British who would not join it. All were killed without mercy and thousands perished.

This uprising in AD 66 was the last real struggle against the invading Romans. By AD 80, a line of forts had been built by Julius Agricola between the Forth and Clyde to keep out the warlike Picts, and it was left to the Emperor Hadrian forty years later to build the massive wall between the Tyne and Solway. Agricola's victories gave Britain a peace that lasted nearly seventy years and it became a province under Roman military rule and administration, along with Gaul and Spain.

Many Britons took easily to the Roman way of life, some gaining high ranks in political, military and civil affairs. The life and customs of the people became much changed.

Parts of the forest were cleared, roads replaced broken tracks, and towns such as Bath, Gloucester, Leicester, Chester, York and Lincoln grew up along these roads, all based on London as the great trading centre. These towns were built in the Roman style and were fortified with mighty walls and castles. It was a time of constant travel, as trade increased and the wealth of the country developed. The Romans were, after all, rulers of the land for some 400 years. However, in the wild spaces of Wales, Devon and Cornwall, the conquest had little lasting effect. This, of course, resulted in a great division between various parts of the country.

As the country became more civilized, mineral mines were actively worked, agriculture flourished and Britain became a great corn-producing country. The skills of British builders and craftsmen were much sought after, many of them travelling abroad to work on the Continent. The higher class of Britons lived side by side with the Romans and it wasn't long before they began to assume their dress, copy their mode of life and even to speak their language. They kept in close touch with the outer world and its events and became prosperous and wealthy. But at the same time, the Britons of the countryside clung to their own language and customs and sank almost into serfdom.

It was during this time that a new religion emerged, that of Christianity, based on the birth, life, death and resurrection of Jesus of Nazareth, born in Bethlehem of Judaea, part of the conquered Roman province of Palestine. His many followers, convinced by his teachings, continued his work and within a few short years the new ideas grew and flourished, spreading to all parts of the world. It was inevitable that news of this religion should reach Britain, and it was at this time that the Glastonbury legend evolved. It is said that Joseph of Arimathea came to Britain about the year AD 62 when, on thrusting his rod into the ground, it is said it budded into a blossoming thorn, flowering at Christmas-time. Whilst there is no corroborating knowledge that Joseph of Arimathea actually came to this country he could well have done so, as indeed could St Paul himself, for it is known he travelled extensively carrying his missionary message to 'the farthest limits of the west'.

During the second century, persecution of the Christians in Gaul drove many from their lands and it is more than probable that some found refuge in Britain. It is known that by the beginning of the third century there were many Christians in this country, and around AD 33 we learn of St Alban becoming the first Christian martyr in Britain. The son of Roman parents living at Verulanium, he was sent to Rome to be educated, returning as an officer of the Roman army in Britain. He was rich and popular, and welcomed scholars and travellers from many countries to his home. Such activities were somewhat frowned upon by the authorities and at a time when Christians were being persecuted in Rome, the same began to happen in this country. Alban's friendships with all, including Christians, were looked upon with increasing suspicion.

One traveller became Alban's friend, his personality and way of life persuading Alban to join him as a Christian. When the stranger's whereabouts became known, Roman soldiers arrived at Alban's house to arrest the visitor. It wasn't realised until later that the prisoner they took was not the stranger but Alban himself, who'd taken his guest's place. When he too declared himself to be a Christian and refused to offer sacrifice to the Roman Gods, he was tried and tortured and finally condemned to death by beheading. A church was later built over the place where he died, the town becoming known as St Albans.

At this time the Roman occupation was coming to an end with troops being with-drawn and returned to Italy since they were unable continue to afford protection to distant provinces. By the end of AD 409 when the last of the Romans left, the Britons were left in isolation to face a series of savage hordes who began to attack the country towards the latter part of the fourth century. Known throughout history as the Angles, Saxons and Jutes, they came at different times and landed at different places, but each group was intent on winning part of the land for themselves. There were endless struggles, with patches of fierce resistance as the country was ravaged by fire and trampled in battle. It wasn't too long before the country began to fall into the grip of its foreign foes. The invaders swept over the country, wreaking special vengeance on the churches and any vestiges of Christianity they encountered. Christian priests were murdered, crosses were hacked to pieces and any sacred treasures destroyed. The little wooden churches were burned with any who sought refuge in them.

The new gods the invaders introduced were symbolic of their nature. They were relent-less, vengeful and cruel. Among these were Thor the Thunderer, Woden the war god, Tiu the dark god (whom it was considered death to meet) and many others. Although the new priests never really gained the same influence over the people that the Druids had imposed, their rule of terror did weave itself into the ordinary life of the people. This is reflected in much of the language still in use today, particularly so in the names of the days of the week – Tiu's Day, Woden's Day, Thor's Day, and Soetere Day.

Lucy Diamond in her book *How the Gospel Came to Britain* tells us that the Jutes were the first to gain a secure foothold in the country, being helped by the Kentish

Britons themselves. They at first requested the help of their invaders in fighting off the Picts and Scots, but it wasn't long before that assistance was turned against them by the invaders. By AD 473 the Jutes, under their chiefs Hengest and Horsa, had won all of Kent. The Jutes settled there and developed their own laws and civil life.

The Saxons arrived in larger numbers and in different groups. The Middle Saxons forced their way along the Thames and settled around London, the area becoming known as Middlesex. Another group landed in the valleys of the Colne and Stour and captured Colchester, giving us the name Essex, whilst the South Saxons, led by Aella, landed near Selsea Bill, fighting their way eastwards through what had been one of the most Romanised parts of Britain. They captured Anderida, near where Pevensey now stands, slaying all its British defenders until they came to the impenetrable Andredsweald Forest. Here, they found themselves only able to gain a narrow strip of coast where they settled, establishing the kingdom of the South Saxons – Sussex. The most powerful and effective conquest of southern Britain was that of the West Saxons, who landed by Southampton Water. Here they were able to penetrate through the forests towards the interior. Under Cerdic and Cymric they made their way towards Winchester where, in a great battle, they slew thousands of Britons and elected Cerdic as King of Wessex

The Angles landed on the east coast, making their way inland by the rivers. One group, from the south, settled in Suffolk and another, from the north, in Norfolk. Before long the whole of East Anglia, including the east coast, was conquered and settled by them. One group made their way up the River Witham and established themselves near Lindum, calling themselves 'Lindiswaras', meaning dwellers near Lindum – the city now known as Lincoln. Other Angles landed on Holderness, north of the Humber, and within fifty years were in possession of all Yorkshire as far as the Pennine Range. Other groups followed the course of the Trent and the Soar, gradually overrunning the Midlands as far as the border between the Britons and the Welsh. These settlers became known as the Mercians – the men of the Marches or borders. A powerful force of Angles led by Ida raided the north-east coast gaining possession of the land between the sea and the Cheviots where, in the uplands of the Tweed, they founded the Kingdom of Bernicia. Here, in AD 547, Ida built the mighty fortress of Bamborough.

The Britons who escaped this destructive conquest fled to the hills and forests, taking refuge in the wild country spaces to the west – Cornwall, Devon and Somerset, and to Wales and among the Cumbrian hills. Christianity was almost swept away and survived only in the parts where the invader was unable to penetrate. In these distant parts of the country the faith was preserved and in Wales especially it developed a character and standing of its own. The churches here were built safe from outside influences and the clergy made little or no effort to convert their heathen foes.

So although by the middle of the sixth century much of the country had been conquered, roughly all those parts west of the Pennine range, together with North Wales and West Wales (as Devon and Cornwall were then called) were still in British hands and preserved the Christian faith. Later, in AD 577, the West Saxons gained land in the Severn Valley, consequently cutting off those Britons who had fled to Wales, from those in Cornwall. This caused both groups to become isolated, each continuing to hold to their methods of worship, which grew up independently.

During this time the Christian religion was also gaining favour in Ireland where there were scholars and craftsmen who had kept in close contact with the people of Gaul – a kindred race – from the earliest times. From them they learned how to work gold and metal and through the years they developed a native skill that showed itself in original and beautiful designs and exquisite workmanship. However, in Ireland the organisation of the country was still tribal and there was no real town life. The buildings would still have been of wood or wattle-and-daub and even the most important places and centres of rule were little more than rough settlements. Earlier, the Druids there had been highly trained in memorising, and had developed records and some sort of literature from very early days. Although both the Greeks and Romans had known that country it was never conquered and their first important contact came through the introduction of Christianity.

Gradually the whole of Ireland came under Christian rule, especially through the work and teaching of St Patrick. Here too though, the church came to possess a character of its own. Bishops were ordained, with clergy caring for settlements, monasteries grew into schools of learning. These kept alive both Christianity and the arts, poetry and literature at a time when it was almost quenched in Europe.

It was therefore from Ireland that Christianity later returned to Britain. One of the greatest of their missions here was led by Columbia, whose parents were Christians and of royal blood. Columbia was schooled at Noville on Lough Foyle at one of the most famous of the monastic schools in the country. He soon decided the monastic life was for him and, aged about twenty-five, he founded his first monastery. Like St Patrick he travelled a great deal preaching and teaching and setting up monasteries. He founded, amongst others, the house at Kells where the beautiful *Book of Kells* was written. In AD 563 he left Ireland and with a band of devoted helpers reached the rocky island of Iona where he began his work and ministry. His dedication made the tiny island one of the most sacred shrines of Christianity. The settlement prospered and the work grew as Columbia led his missionaries into the heart of the fierce heathen tribes, preaching and baptising. Like other missionaries before him he sifted what was good in the old native lore and incorporated this into his teaching. Thus the northern part of Britain became influenced by Christian principles.

The passing years saw the arrival of other missionaries, not least Augustine who landed in Kent in the year AD 597 and set up Canterbury as a strong centre of Christian and political influence. However, during the seventh century Britain again entered a period of paganism, with wars erupting between various groups as each fought for supremacy. Much of history at this time lies hidden, not for nothing is it known as the 'Dark Ages'. However the flame that had been lit those many years ago, although flickering badly, was never completely extinguished. Thus it was that by medieval times the country was ready and eager to again accept Christianity, and the new missionaries were able to exert a lasting hold on the land.

The Cross Through History

The practice of erecting countryside and churchyard crosses dates back to long before the Christian era for, as we have seen, the early Christians utilised existing traditions and sites in their efforts to convert people to the new way of thinking. This included standing stones that had long been held in reverence. One such example, known as Wergin's Stone, can to be found in fields alongside the main road from Sutton St Nicholas to Hereford. This megalithic structure, standing some 6ft high, has an irregular base and appears to be unworked, apart from a cavity thought to be for offerings or tribute. Mr Watkins, in his book *The Old Straight Track* states that almost all waysides and churchyard crosses evolve from earlier mark stones and this particular stone could well have originated as an ancient boundary stone, although its true origins are unknown. Today it is protected by metal railings. It is also thought that the churchyard cross at Vowchurch, which aligns with a ford over the little river, probably stands on an unhewn markstone.

As time passed, many of these pre-historic stones took on a new importance. For example the Stone of Scone was brought to London and placed beneath the chair on which kings and queens were crowned at Westminster, remaining there for many years. Of even earlier usage was the Coronation Stone at Kingston-on-Thames, where six Saxon kings were crowned. It seems that upright columns, often described as a link between Father God and Mother Earth, have long been regarded as phallic symbols. Many early stones resemble a human phallus in the same way that early Mother Earth statuettes portrayed a heavily pregnant mother.

Such stones were not only regarded as religious symbols but also, in many cases, played an important role in the life of the community – with some growing in importance politically. Various secular meetings were held either at the spot where they had been erected or in their vicinity. These would occasionally take the form of legal assemblies. For example, itinerant justices sat at the cross in the Strand in London, which later became the site of the church of St Mary-le-Strand. In Owen's *Old Stone Crosses* there is a report of farm workers in Wales who would gather at the town cross in order to be hired, when the rate of pay was fixed, this being known as 'the cross wage'.

Owing to the fact that folk neither understood the meaning of the early standing stones nor could imagine how they came to be where they were, it was inevitable that various superstitious rituals grew up around them, resulting in many folk myths.

Wergin's Stone near the Sutton St Nicholas/ Hereford road.

For example, at Rudstone in Humberside there is in the churchyard, the largest standing stone in Britain. At 6ft wide and more than 25ft high, it weighs some twenty-six tonnes. Composed of millstone grit, the nearest supply of which is at least ten miles away, it probably dates from about 2000 BC. As with most of the old standing stones, since people were mystified about them they treated them with awe, not to mention wonder and fear. The majority of the myths that grew up around the stones were connected to the eternal battle between good and evil, between God and the Devil. In this instance it is said the evil one was so enraged that a church be built within his jurisdiction that he hurled a stone javelin, missing the building by just a few feet.

Superstition and myth continued for many centuries and as late as the nineteenth century coffins continued to be taken three times around the churchyard cross in Manaton, Devon, much to the annoyance of the vicar who preached against this. In desperation he eventually broke up the cross and hid the pieces. In her book *Folklore of Herefordshire* Mrs Leather mentions that at Brilley, the coffin was carried three times round the stone in the belief that it would prevent the Devil obtaining the souls of the deceased. At this time most burials took place inside the church, the wealthier parishioners having a memorial either on the wall or set into it. When this custom fell from use and internment took place in the churchyard, a memorial on the outside wall of the church would be the ultimate status symbol.

A special treasure in this church is the wooden ceiling at the east end of the chancel, which is known as a bladachino. Its beams date from the fifteenth century, although the border is later. Such ceilings were erected to keep the dust from the altar; Cromwell later decided such features should be ripped out. Brilley and Michaelchurch are therefore the only churches in the diocese to retain them, probably due to the remoteness of the area.

At the crossroads between Moreton Hampstead and North Bovey, also in Devon, tradition has it that when the church clock chimes midnight, the cross there known as Stumpy Cross, is said to revolve three times and there are many tales of stones moving by themselves. At the top of Bredon Hill in Worcestershire there is what is locally known as

Monolith in the churchyard at Rudstone, Humberside.

The cross in Brilley churchyard, Herefordshire, later used as a sundial.

the 'elephant stone' since from some directions it gives the appearance of such an animal, although its correct name should rightly be the Bambury Stone. There is a local superstition that the elephant will, when it hears the bells of Pershore Abbey peeling at midnight, come into the valley to drink the waters of the River Avon.

There are many other stories throughout the country telling of ancient stones said to move under their own volition. For example, it is believed that Wergin's Stone, already mentioned, suddenly moved 240 paces from its former position some time in 1652. Nobody could think how this could have occurred since it needed nine yoke of oxen to return it to its original position. There are also two stories of moving stones in Gloucestershire. The Tingle Stone at the long barrow near Avening is said to run round the field when it hears the clock strike midnight, whilst the Long Stone at Minchinhampton does likewise, also when the clock strikes twelve.

In Druid times crossroads were held to be sacred spots and were often marked by upright or cushion-shaped stones, as were wells and springs. Such stones were naturally utilised by the early Christians, who chiselled Christian symbols in relief on them. Since pagan Saxons worshipped stone pillars, so early Christian missionaries, in addition to using the old stones, would erect their own stone crosses, carving on them figures of Christ and his apostles. Prior to the building of churches, these would have been used as locations for preaching, baptising and the saying of Mass.

The earliest crosses were therefore probably just simple stones incised with Christian symbols or had crosses in relief placed upon them, whilst marker stones have sometimes been used as a base or socket-stone for a later cross. In our Three Counties we have an example at Pembridge in Herefordshire, where the market house was erected alongside an ancient marker stone, and there are examples of other marker stones being used as the foundation of later churchyard or preaching crosses.

At Pembridge, an attractive 'black & white' village where the community has long been known for its breed of Hereford cattle, it was inevitable that a market should be set up to deal with their sale. This must have long witnessed the coming and going of numerous drovers and herds over the years. The market house that came to be erected later is of plain construction, with eight oak pillars bearing notches where planks of wood would rest to enable folk to display their wares, and supporting a stone-tiled roof. Next to one of the pillars, which itself is said to rest on the base of a medieval cross, is an unworked cushion-shaped stone, originally a meeting place on a track. This must have decided the site of the market and shows the progression from an early way-mark stone to the finished market house.

As the early missionaries travelled, they set up centres where folk could gather, build communities and worship as they wished. These early Christian preachers no doubt had great difficulty in weaning folk from their pagan beliefs, resulting in their attempts to accept those beliefs that could be reinterpreted with a Christian meaning. They thus began to take over pagan sites, endowing them with Christian symbols and ideas. As they moved about the country preaching Christianity, they used natural objects such as springs, trees and standing stones already regarded as sacred to the community, to convey their new message, and where they met people worshipping heathen images they would give these a Christian context. Some of the pagan gods and goddesses were even adopted and canonised as Christian saints. Brid became St Bridget or St Bride, Ma and Matrona became Mary, Santon the Holy Fire became St Anne and Sinclair the Holy Light became St Clare.

Pembridge Market house, Herefordshire.

Many Christian churches were built on pagan sites and many of the menhirs, monoliths and stones formerly used for pagan worship were later dedicated to Christian use, as were wells and other items held sacred in early times, with many churches being erected on the foundations of old temples. Places of worship in the earliest time were, in the main, of circular construction. The Druid's standing stones were arranged thus, as were temples and Christian rotundas such as the Holy Sepulchre at Jerusalem, a Constantinian building. The Knights Templar also built the majority of their churches to a circular design, as can be seen at Garway in Herefordshire where relatively recent excavations have revealed the foundations of the original church. Therefore, churches found in circular graveyards may indicate that they were built on sites that were originally pagan.

There are many early crosses in the north of England, some fashioned by St Wilfred, Archbishop of York, in the eighth century. It was known that St Wilfred took stonecutters who worked crosses on a spot chosen and consecrated by him, with him when he travelled. These works fall mainly under four schools of art – Celtic, Saxon, Roman and Scandinavian. The majority of these consist of interlacing scroll-work with knotted and interlaced cords in various designs, the most popular being vine and rope work.

It is extremely difficult today to interpret many of the symbols and carvings made on these stones, especially since time has resulted in their defacement. They can range from the inconsequential doodlings of those working them, to theories involving mystical and/or folklore significance, and it is thought that many crosses may bear writings or messages that we are unable to recognise or decipher at the present time. For example, is the typical interlaced Celtic design just a version of the twisting and knotting of cords as used as a sacred 'language' in other various countries, or is it purely an intricate pattern?

The cross in several forms is an ancient symbol that pre-dated Christianity, one of the earliest being the swastika. In India and the Orient the swastika represented the sacred fire and fruitfulness and was known as a symbol of good luck. It is also a symbol of the sun and has been found in Hindu carvings, in South American rock carvings and on Central American pottery. This is now little seen other than on old Christian monuments in Rome, due mainly to its later use by Adolf Hitler when he cleverly changed the direction of the points, debasing this ancient symbol of life into one portraying tyranny, conquest and pride. On the other hand, another cross, the ankh or ansa, which originally symbolised the lion-headed goddess of vengeance and conquest, later became a sign for life and the living.

The cross thus appears in many forms in different civilizations but is Christianity's most important symbol. When associated with the death of Christ it is a symbol of sadness and melancholy but in earlier times it symbolised the combining of God and Earth and was a sign of harmony. It has been said that early Christians preferred as their symbol the anchor, fish or chi-rho (a monogram of the first two letters of Christ's name in Greek), the cross not being referred to. It was only later, in the fifth century when Christians began to think through the implications of the crucifixion, that they begin to regard the cross as their symbol.

However, in his book *Old Times*, Walter Clifford Meller tells us that one Tertullian, writing as early as AD 199 states that at that time Christians would mark the sign of the cross on their foreheads 'at every commencement of business, whenever we go in or come out of any place, when we dress for a journey, when we go into a bath, when we go to meat, when lights are brought in, when we lie down or sit down and whatever business we have.' This rather disputes the thought that the cross was not regarded as a favourite Christian symbol until later. A later writer, St Chrysostom, says in AD 350 that crosses were erected in numerous places, writing that, 'In the private houses, in the public market-places, in the desert, on the highway, on mountains, on hills, on the sea, on ships, on islands, there are crosses.'

The cross was usually one of two kinds. The first of these is the Greek cross with all sides of the same length, sometimes flared at the end and often appearing within a circle. It is known that Constantine, the first Christian Emperor, arranged for his soldiers to carry this symbol on their shields. The second type was the Latin cross – a vertical shaft with a horizontal bar two thirds up the shaft, as is now usually used. Apparently this was thought to be the best suited to take the body of Christ, even though it's more than likely that the cross on which Christ died was a simple stake or T cross.

The plain, or empty cross, is one without the figure of Jesus on it and signifies an image of God's power and hope, whilst a crucifix is a cross to which the body of Jesus is fixed or superimposed. Again this appears in many different forms. In early times Jesus is usually shown as being in the prime of life and he was usually draped, with his face portrayed as beardless, his head erect. He may be shown with his arms outstretched and wearing a long seamless tunic (an alb), or perhaps wearing a halo or gold crown. The word alb was taken from the Latin *albus* meaning white and signifying purity of heart. It was a vestment worn by the priest during the celebration of the Mass. He may also be shown with outstretched arms blessing followers or with open hands in an attitude of benediction.

These early portraits were most popular between the sixth and thirteenth centuries when artists preferred to show Jesus as wearing clothes, and it is thought it was not until the time of the Black Death that carvings of a naked and bearded figure appeared. Later crucifixes depicted Jesus' suffering, when he appears naked and wearing a crown of thorns with nails through his palms and crossed feet, and with a cut just below the ribs showing where he was speared whilst hanging on the cross. One of the earliest of this type is to be seen at Kilmartin in Argyllshire, where the cross shows an undraped figure with his head bent sorrowfully, without crown or halo, short-haired and beardless. On the other side of this cross-shaft however, there are faint traces of a fullydraped figure with his hands raised in blessing, the position of the feet suggesting a seated figure.

As the cross symbol advanced it began to be shown in many different ways. For example, a squared cross within a circle is known as a Celtic or wheel-headed one, whilst an Easter cross is garlanded by flowers, in particular the lily (or more recently the daffodil). Crosses terminating in the form of a fleur-de-lis are known as a cross-fleury, whilst one that is notched at equal distances all round is known as a reguly cross. One appearing like a 'T' is a Tau cross, originally the Egyptian cross of life. This reflects a debate in the early church on the proper shape of a cross, and became associated with the fourth-century desert hermit St Anthony, an Egyptian said to be the founder of the monastic system.

A cross with four small ones within its arms is known as a Jerusalem cross – the five crosses symbolising the five wounds of Christ. This was the insignia of the Crusaders, the Pope having allowed the Knights Templars, a military knightly organisation, to wear a blood-red cross as a symbol of martyrdom. The black and white cross of the same form, known as a Maltese cross and used by the St John's organisation, was originally used by

Caedmon's Cross, Whitby, Yorkshire, *c.* 1910.

the Knight Hospitallers who, at the start of the Crusades, tended to sick pilgrims. It is said the eight-pointed cross symbolises the eight beatitudes in Matthew and is an emblem of love. Later this order also became more military and was finally expelled from Rhodes by the Turks, whence they settled in Malta in the early fifteenth century.

In the life of the present-day church, a cross may have up to three bars symbolising (from the bottom) faith, hope and love. When carried in procession a single bar signifies a bishop, a double bar an archbishop and three bars (or the inscription UNRI crossbar and footrest), the Pope. The Patriarchal cross of the Eastern Church has two bars for the inscription and crossbar.

The elaborately sculptured crosses erected by the Saxons date from the seventh century, with many being found in the Scottish border country. One of the oldest is from Ruthwell, now in Durham Cathedral Museum. In the panels are sculptures representing events in the life of Christ. The lowest panel is too defaced to know what it portrays, but the second shows the flight into Egypt. The third shows St Paul, and the fourth is Christ treading the heads of swine beneath his feet. On the highest is the figure of St John the Baptist with a lamb, whilst the reverse side shows the annunciation, the salutation and other scenes of gospel history. The two narrower sides are covered with floral patterns and other decorations.

In addition to the figures are five stanzas of an Anglo Saxon poem that tells the story of the crucifixion from the point of view of the cross itself – from the time when it was a growing tree until after the body of Christ had been taken down for burial. On the head of the cross it says 'Caedmon made me'. He is reputed to be the first English poet, becoming a monk in mature years after having been a swineherd. He is said to have had no education until then, but his later life was spent writing poems on religious themes. A cross outside the abbey at Whitby in Yorkshire commemorates his life.

3

The Cross Gains Strength

It is thought that crosses were first introduced in the south and west of the country and from there they travelled slowly northwards. Since many of these were of wood they have disappeared over time, but many still remain throughout the country. The majority of the Cornish churches were founded between 500-800 AD, and this part of the country contains a great number of these ancient crosses, many dating back to the eighth century. Although built of very hard stone, today many are little more than rough stumps showing little or no carving. They having been almost obliterated by the passage of time and most are quite small. The Cornish word for cross is 'crowz', 'crows' or 'crowse' and place names incorporating these words can usually be taken to be ancient, as they will probably have sprung up about such a landmark

As has been seen, it was undoubtedly extremely difficult to persuade folk to completely forsake their earlier pagan beliefs, and as late as the eleventh century King Canute felt obliged to pass a law forbidding 'every heathenism'. These included worshipping the sun, moon, fire, rivers, water-wells, stones or forest trees of any kind, also 'any love of witchcraft or the promoting of morthwork' – 'morth' being the Norman word for secret killings.

The Welsh and Cornish Britons, being in the remoter parts of the country, remained separate from the Saxons until the time of the Norman Conquest, when their lands were appropriated and divided amongst the Norman chiefs, although it is thought the majority of their monuments remained almost undisturbed. These early Christians, living in isolated parts, continued to worship very much in their old ways and this can be seen in particular at the church dedicated to St Dubricious, or Dyfric to give him his Welsh name, at Hentland in Herefordshire. Although something of a legend, and the facts are difficult to sift from the fiction, he was an influential figure in the fifth and sixth centuries.

He was born at nearby Madley, so was closely associated with the area in the old province of Arkenfield which was a bastion of the old British church founded in the third century during the Roman occupation. Being on the borders of Wales and extremely isolated, it had maintained its faith and traditions against the invading Anglo-Saxons. There are four local churches dedicated to him, but Hentland was particularly important as St Dubricious founded a teaching monastery at Llanfrother, one and a half miles to

Hentland, Herefordshire, where the early form of
British Christianity remained unchanged for centuries
prior to the Norman Conquest.

the north of the church. Here, it is reported that over 2,000 students passed through his monastery and were sent to preach the gospel all over Wales and the west of England. Dubricious became the first Bishop of Llandaff, and Hentland was part of his See. Later, as Archbishop of Caerleon and Primate of the West British Church, legend has it that he officiated at the crowning of King Arthur in AD 313.

In 1128 the first Superior of the Knights Templars, Hugh de Poyens, visited England and he granted land in Cornwall to this group. There are great similarities between the crosses of Ireland and Cornwall, which is hardly surprising bearing in mind these latter were probably originally set up by missionaries from Ireland. Certainly the oldest known crosses in the country lie outside our local area, although there are part-stones to be found inside several churches here, such as that at Tenbury Wells, Mickleton and Cropthorne in Worcestershire, and Newent in Gloucestershire.

Although many crosses are in churchyards, others appear to have been randomly set up. One of the oldest of these is to be found at Million. Another of the oldest Cornish crosses is that of St Peran which stands near the ruins of a deserted church amid the sand hills of Perranporth. This is mentioned in a charter of King Edgar in AD 960 and was an old landmark even then. The early Christians continued this fashion of setting up stones, although these usually differ from the older ones by being smaller and bearing inscriptions.

Of the very early crosses, the majority are memorials erected to chieftains or other important personages, with many displaying myths and Viking stories that were told in stone.

Two pillars at Sandbach in Cheshire are said to be the oldest Christian relics in England. Reputedly, these were erected in the eighth century on the spot where a priest from Northumberland first preached Christianity. Made of very hard Silurian stone, the scenes on the large cross show scenes that are scriptural, whilst those on the small one display

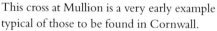

This cross at Mullion is a very early example typical of those to be found in Cornwall.

Another early Cornish cross to be found at Perranporth.

secular history. On the lower part of the east side of the higher cross there is a circle, thought to signify the salutation of Elizabeth. At the foot of the cross are figures of Mary, wife of Cleophas, and Mary Magdalene with symbols for the evangelists – an angel for St Matthew, a lion for St Mark, a bull for St Luke and an eagle for St John. The sides bear carvings and filigree work.

The figures on the small cross seem to represent Peda setting out from Mercia to seek the hand of Alchfleda, King Ossy's daughter. Both crosses were mutilated and knocked down during the Puritan era, which must have taken some violence for the larger one has torn away a great part of the socket-stone in which it was fixed. Fragments were then used as the sides of a well and some parts were taken to Oulton Park, a stately home nearby belonging to Sir Philip de Malpas Egerton, in order to adorn a grotto. It is believed a Colonel Forde, the Lord of the Manor of Sandbach, was responsible for collecting the pieces of the large cross, whilst the shorter was restored by a Mr Palmer of Manchester. Both crosses would have terminated in a cross and circle, similar to other Celtic ones.

Many of these early crosses, especially of the wheel-headed Celtic type, are commemorative. As a general rule, a cross within a circle is older than one out of a circle. There is an eleventh-century cross near Carew Castle in Pembrokeshire commemorating a King Maredudd. This has an eastern influence – its counterpart can be found in old metalwork and carvings from Cairo or Central America. It is 14ft high and shows a variety of designs. On the top panel is a swastika. At the foot of this cross, the bottom panel shows a very

These two crosses at Sandbach in Cheshire are said to be the oldest in the country.

clever interlaced design – a continuous ribbon with no ending, which, when traced around, returns to its starting point. It is thought this may have had a special meaning, conveying a message to the initiated when it was originally carved.

Another very early example is Muiredach's Cross at Monsterboice in County Louth. Muiredach was abbot of the monastery here from AD 890-923 and the elaborately carved cross, dating from the tenth century, would originally have been coloured. The carving shows scriptural and other scenes with a series of patterns, whilst the head is shaped as a shingle-roofed church. The whole cross stands 17ft 8in tall.

With the cross being held in such high reverence during the early days, it is little wonder that throughout Christendom the erection of crosses occurred so often, and appeared in so many styles with differing designs and uses. Mr Meller tells us that crosses had Imperial sanction, for in AD 324-37, the Emperor Constantine passed an edict, ordering that crosses be erected along the public highways where in pagan times had stood statues of the gods defining different territories and properties.

Yet still the old pagan ways continued. In AD 452 a further edict was passed ruling that 'if any infidel either lighted ruches (sic), or worshipped trees, fountains or stones, or neglected to destroy them, he should be found guilty of sacrilege', whilst in AD 567 the Council of Tours recommended excommunication of those who 'persisted in worshipping trees, stones or fountains'. But stone worship was still a problem a 100 years later. A decree of Nantes in AD 658 stated bishops and their servants should 'dig up and remove and hide to places where they cannot be found, those stones which in remote and woody places are still worshipped and where vows are still made'.

Another example of a Cornish cross, to be found at Carew.

The elaborately carved St Boyne's Cross at Monasterboice in Ireland.

In the tenth century Dunstan was appointed Abbot of Canterbury and his regime brought about a revival in monastic ways. Benedictine monks were introduced into the existing abbeys and under Wessex's King Edgar, a document called the *Regularis Concordia* attempted to regularise the structure of behaviour and worship throughout the country. But it was not until after the successful invasion by the Normans in 1066 that great changes began to take place. The old wooden churches were replaced by stone buildings and during the next two centuries great new churches and cathedrals came into being. Norman barons built such places of worship on lands awarded to them by William as a reward for their support during the Conquest.

Thus it was in Medieval times that the majority of churchyard crosses were erected, and by the time of the Reformation there are thought to have been some 5,000 in England alone. Some churches had several, such as at Ilkley in Yorkshire where there are three, as also at Whalley in Lancashire. Two of the latter acted for a long time as gateposts, their use for this purpose probably commencing during the time of the Puritans.

Old churchyard and village crosses come in various shapes and forms, although in the majority of cases these are set on steps, three being the most frequent number signifying the Father, Son and Holy Ghost. Five steps would signify the five wounds of Christ and eight the beatitudes. On occasions the shaft was extremely high and the cross itself very small. Occasionally, Medieval cross sculptures were sculpted from living nude models, one such instance being that at the Cistercian abbey of Meaux near Beverley in the East Riding of Yorkshire, where the abbot records, 'The artist of this never worked at any fine or important part of it except on Fridays, fasting on bread and water, and he had all the time a naked man under his eyes, and he laboured to give to his crucifix the beauty of the model.'

Crosses in this country, as opposed to practices abroad, seem nearly always to have been placed in, or close to, towns, abbeys and churches. Even in the case of the Eleanor crosses (about which more later), these were erected in the towns and not along the roads along which her bier was carried.

Crosses today can be found in the most unlikely places, such as alongside tracks and in hidden places. Local place names will often suggest where earlier crosses existed – in particular the words 'crucis' (as in Ampney Crucis, where the latter Latin word means 'of the cross') or 'Cros' (as in Crosby, Cumbria). Names referring to churches, abbeys and priories, friars, nuns or monks may well indicate that at the least, such towns and villages were home to such establishments in the past and so could well have had crosses nearby.

Whilst place names can often give an insight into the past and those utilising the word 'cross' could well indicate there was once such a one in the vicinity, such names could also refer to a crossroads. However, as these themselves were often marked by standing crosses there could well have been one in the area in the past. Usually if the place name has as its prefix a Christian name, such as that of 'Patty's Cross' near Leominster in Herefordshire, this could well suggest such an erection once stood there, although again this was not always the case.

In several parts of the country there are places called Cross-in-Hand, there being four in Herefordshire, also one at Tenbury in Worcestershire and a Cross Hands in Gloucestershire. However, all these seem to refer to road junctions. They could also refer to the custom of criminals forswearing the kingdom, who were protected on their journey by wearing a white robe and holding a white cross of wood, often referred to as a cross-in-hand. It could well be that refuge stations or crosses passed on the highway would be known by this appellation.

Our area was rich in abbeys and their associated buildings. In Gloucestershire there were eight – at Cirencester, Deerhurst, Gloucester, Kingswood, Leonard Stanley, Prinknash, Quenington and Tewkesbury. In Worcesterhire there were also eight – at Astley, Cock Hill, Dudley, Evesham, Halesowen, Little Malvern, Pershore and Worcester itself. There were even more in Herefordshire – at Abbey Dore, Aconbury, Belmont, Craswall, Flamesford, Garway, Hereford, Ledbury, Leominster, Limebrook, Monkland, Shobden and Wigmore. The connection between crown and church was immensely strong, with most of the administration of the country being undertaken under the juris-diction of the clergy. With such a high number of abbey houses in the Three Counties it was inevitable they should become such a force in the land.

Many crosses disappeared relatively recently. As towns began to grow in the eighteenth and nineteenth centuries these were found to be in the way of roads or buildings. In their book *Vanishing England* P.H. Ditchfield and Fred Roe tell us that at Colne complaints were made that 'there was no room for coaches to turn, and idlers congregated on the steps'. It was also said to interfere with business, so in 1882 their cross was simply swept away. In Lancashire, a zealous Protestant vicar, regarding such items as being products of the Catholic Church, made it his mission to destroy as many as he could, foretelling the deaths of any who protested. When several of his prophecies coincidentally came true, folk became increasingly scared of arguing with him!

Other early crosses disappeared with time, in particular those that had wooden shafts, which naturally deteriorated far more quickly. However, these can often be recognised, as in many cases remains appear in socket holes or on the top step. In addition, in most cases the socket hole is smaller than would have been the case for a stone shaft. Small holes can be found at Ganarew, Linton, Goodrich and Docklow, all in Herefordshire, amongst others. It would seem that if these shafts held any figures or cross-heads these would also have been of wood. This was certainly the case at Craswall, Michaelchurch Escley, Middleton and St Margarets, where fragments have been found remaining in the socket holes. It is also possible that if wooden cross shafts were smaller than the hole it would be possible to fit them loosely in any stone socket bases, making for easy removal to enable them to be carried in processions. Wooden crosses and gravestones are, of course, being erected on occasion to this day. One thinks especially of the many small wooden crosses marking the deaths of soldiers during the First World War.

4

Parliamentary Times

During the 1600s the situation throughout the country became extremely complicated and disorganised. James I, on becoming King of England in 1603 enforced severe laws against Catholics and everybody was ordered to attend Anglican services or be fined. When Charles I succeeded James he found himself embroiled in great religious and political upheaval. In 1642, the Civil War broke out. Eventually, in 1644 a Parliamentary army led by Oliver Cromwell defeated a Royalist army at Marston Moor and Parliament reorganised itself into the New Model Army. Charles later fell into the hands of the Scots who handed him over to Parliament. He was tried for treason, found guilty by a special court and beheaded. For the next eleven years the country was ruled as a republic, with Cromwell in the position of Lord Protector.

In the main, the Civil War came about through religious disagreements, with many seeking a simpler, purer form of worship. This eventually led to a fanatical wish to destroy anything that smacked of Catholicism, resulting in anything previously used by them being regarded as idolatry. This resulted in an act of Parliament being passed on 26 August 1643 decreeing that all 'altars and communion tables, images and pictures of saints, or superstitious inscriptions in churches, chapels and other places of public prayers and churchyards' were to be destroyed. They went further, forbidding tapers, candlesticks, crucifixes, crosses and all images and pictures of any one or more persons of the Trinity or of the Virgin Mary. Altar rails were to be destroyed and the ground where they'd been was to be levelled, whilst stained-glass windows were to be smashed.

So fanatical were they that a further act was passed a year later on 9 May 1644 confirming this but taking the orders further, to include additionally the destruction of even frames or cases where images stood, together with organs, copes, surplices and religious vestments, roods and fonts.

The destruction of the crosses usually took the form of knocking off the head and, in many cases, mutilating the shaft. Usually these heads were broken up but in some cases they were hidden or buried. At Madley, Tyberton, Hentland, Putley, Kings Caple and Knill the tops of crosses have been found and replaced on their broken shafts. One, at Tedstone Delamere, has been inserted into a wall by the lych-gate to the churchyard, where a glass enclosure protects the original head, allowing it to be seen from both sides. This bears a carving of the crucifixion on one side and the Virgin and Child on

The cross in the churchyard at
Sellack, Herefordshire.

the other. In this sculpture Christ has his arms outstretched on a plain cross and wears
a loin cloth.

However we do know of two heads in this area that were allowed to remain – those at
Bosbury and Sellack. The story goes that at the latter, Parliamentary soldiers leaving Ross
with the intention of following orders to destroy the Cross found themselves so hospita-
bly greeted by the vicar that they desisted.

The 1980 Bosbury Church Guide tells us that tradition has it that when Puritan
troops were sent to deface the cross, declaring it to be a Popish symbol, the vicar pleaded
with them to spare it, pointing out it was a Christian symbol. The soldiers thus agreed
to leave the cross provided the words 'Honour not the + but honour God for Christ'
were engraved on the arms. The first four words appear on one side with the remainder
on the other, it still being possible to make out some of the inscription. This cross can
be found to the south of the church by the edge of the path from the lych-gate. Made
of red sandstone, it has a well-proportioned twentieth-century shaft rising to a height
of some 16ft. This rises from a substantial base bearing perpendicular moulding on three
steps and is surmounted by a cross. It is also recorded that an ancient stone was discovered in 1796. Since it was at this date that the churchyard cross was moved, it appears
likely that this had been incorporated in the base of the cross and cropped to fit the
available space.

Following the destruction of crosses, the mutilated shaft was often pressed into service
as a sundial. The earliest example in this area would seem to be that at Weston Beggard,
where it is affixed to the top of the socket-stone and dated 1649. In the early 1920s this
supported a shaft with, alongside this, a 4½in square sundial plate. This date is quite early,
and shows how quickly some churches obeyed the Long Parliament order to destroy
crosses. Apparently, the shaft was later demolished by a storm in November 1928 and
today the top of the socket-stone itself bears the large square sundial plaque covering the

Above: Bosbury Cross, Herefordshire, *c.* 1910.

Left: The cross in its current position.

hole left by its demolition, which could have been moved from elsewhere. This has an elaborate incised metal face bearing its date, the times clearly marked around the edge within a double circle. It also has a childlike drawing of a smiling sun.

Vicars and others receiving their orders carried them out as their consciences allowed. In a few cases they were obeyed to the letter but in many, items were hidden. A good example of this is the aforementioned cross at Ampney Crucis in Gloucestershire. Dedicated to the Holy Rood, this fourteenth-century cross was saved from damage by

The cross at Western Beggard, Herefordshire, lost its shaft many years ago and has had the socket hole covered by a sundial.

church members who walled it inside the rood loft staircase. It has a solid tabernacle-type top with a dog kennel-style roof. Due to a carving of a man in armour on one side, it can be seen that it dates from the first years of Henry V's reign.

The tapering octagonal shaft rises from a solid block of stone and two square steps (7ft 6in and 5ft respectively) and now stands in the village churchyard. The head was replaced on its pedestal in 1860 by Reverend Canon Howman, after it had been found twenty years earlier in rubble in the rood loft of the church, probably having been hidden there to avoid destruction. Due to this care the cross is still in good condition, although time and weather are having an effect. However, in the church itself are detailed drawings of its four faces. The head is divided into four niches and supported by carved Gothic buttresses between which are figures sculptured in relief. One of these reliefs depicts the Virgin Mary and the Christ child. The others contain a crucifix with the figures of St John and Mary, an individual in canon's dress and a knight in armour.

This Cross at Ampney Crucis, Gloucestershire, was saved from destruction in the rood loft staircase and was recovered and reinstated in the churchyard in the 1860s.

Nearby, at the foot of Church Walk, a narrow lane leading from the church, there are two steps with the base and part of the shaft of another old cross, thought to possibly be older than that in the churchyard. In the nearby village of Ampney St Peter there are the remains of another cross.

In order to obey Cromwell's ruling, many of the early crosses were converted to other uses. Congregations would be seen to be obeying the rules if the head was removed, the steps and socket-stones being allowed to remain. A fine example of this can be seen at Shelsea Beauchamp. Here, the cross having been despoiled, there is now a typically shaped sundial rising from the original circular base on four steps, now clothed by flowers. Unfortunately its gnomon (or pointer) is missing but this rests in the church vestry.

When such churches were threatened by the more or less wholesale destruction of their ancient treasures, many congregations, usually under the guidance of their vicars, proceeded to save as much as possible of the building's treasures. Smaller items were removed to dwelling houses, fonts were used as garden features, altar stones removed to churchyards, and wall paintings whitewashed or plastered over. The items that fared the worst were the roods and the screens on or over which these were erected.

The rood (from the Middle English 'rod' or Saxon 'roda' meaning cross) consisted of a large wooden statue showing the crucified Christ, usually with the Virgin Mary on one side and St John on the other. This stood on or above a rood screen that separated the nave (or place of the people) from the chancel containing the sanctuary (the place of the priesthood). The screen replaced the early Middle Age practice of having two pulpits, one either side of the choir that were used for readings at the Eucharist. Above the screen was a loft used in the same way for readings and the chanting of the Gospel. Access to the

Nearby, also at Ampney Crucis, are the remains of what is supposed to be an even earlier cross.

The cross at Shelsea Beauchamp received typical treatment at the time of Oliver Cromwell when it was turned into a sundial.

space at the top of the screen was reached by a staircase, usually built in a pillar at one side, many remains of which can still be seen today. Occasionally, the space where the doorway led through, still exists, often with remnants of stone steps leading to it, appearing rather incongruously in the wall – a doorway to nowhere. Some roods and screens have been lost through later religious intolerance during the Reformation but the majority disappeared during the Civil War. Since, in parish churches, many rood screens were of wood these were easily destroyed and used in other ways, with many of the flimsier screens that were erected between the nave and chancel at this time using wood from the original rood screen.

Although there are very few rood screens remaining in the country, one of the best preserved is that at St Margarets in Herefordshire – a magnificent example of Tudor craftsmanship. The loft, in the form of a gallery, can be climbed into by a series of steps built into the wall, as was common in the majority of churches in the past. This screen would have held a large crucifix, whilst at the top of the two supporting columns two niches would have held figures of the Virgin Mary and St John. At festivals they would have been dressed with nosegays and garlands, but during Lent were covered with veils. The front of the loft is divided into twenty simple, moulded panels – reminiscent of the fine post and panel screens found in old houses – whilst the upper and lower rails of the loft are decorated with running vine foliage friezes and brattishing.

The underside (Soffit) of the loft is coved and divided into panels by moulded ribs meeting at right-angles with bosses at the intersections. These bosses are all different and include men's heads (one with his tongue out), lions, interlaced knots, foliage, a cross on a shield and other devices. At one time the screen would have been richly painted and gilded, but today appears as naturally golden.

One of the very few rood lofts still in existence is that at St Margarets in Herefordshire.

The Middle Ages was an era of faith, with good and evil living side-by-side; the Devil was regarded as much of a force as God. Folk believed fervently in the powers of the bones and other relics of saints, the sanctity of the church and its clergy, the force of good and evil and the omnipresence of God. Likewise they believed sincerely in the Devil, and superstition was rife. After all, if everything that was good came from God, it stood to reason that anything bad must emanate from the Devil. This resulted in things ancient, unexplainable and unknown being regarded with fear and dread. Crosses were therefore regarded in the main as something to be held in awe and respect, although some folk – attempting to prove how brave they were – would ignore the legends.

In 1642, a cross on the bowling green at Whalley in Lancashire fell and a local strong man was asked to remove it. As he did so his foot slipped and the cross fell on him, crushing him to death. This so frightened a neighbour that he confessed that he, together with the dead man, was responsible for having toppled the cross in the first place, believing there might be treasure beneath it. An example of a folk myth attached to the site of an old cross is a story found at Rudhall, Herefordshire. Here, the cross is to be found in a private garden and whilst in a hollow (prior to its being set up on steps) the owner found his gardeners had twice attempted to dig under it to see what was there. Watkins also tells us that when he first saw the cross base at Kingstone in the same county it was partially dug all round where 'treasure hunters' had attempted to burrow beneath it. A further superstition relates to the White Cross where, it was believed, old Taylor's ghost would wander, due to the fact that he'd moved a landmark. Apparently two great stones were then moved to lay the ghost. Another belief was that if one wanted to 'make the acquaintance of Old Nick, one should go to Weobley Churchyard at midnight and walk slowly round the preaching cross seven times, saying the Lord's Prayer backwards' when he would immediately appear.

On other occasions crosses or stones were removed to be used elsewhere. A farmer once moved a boundary stone thinking it would make a handy shelf in his buttery. However, anything put on it was said to have danced about all night, spilling its contents and utterly unnerving the family. Apparently at the wife's insistence, the stone was replaced in its original spot, after which it remained undisturbed.

The passage of time would see many crosses removed or disbursed for a variety of reasons. At Denbigh on the Welsh border, the cross was used as a base for street lighting, whilst shafts were used as gate or other posts. Crosses without heads were turned into sundials or were replaced by inappropriate tops such as that at Childswickham, Worcestershire where, when the eroded thin stone cross fell off in the eighteenth century, it was replaced by an urn. This cross now stands opposite the church on what was once the main road of the village.

In many cases only the stump remains, as at Didmarton, Gloucestershire, where a few feet of the shaft stands on a square base edged at the corners by weatherworn figures. This in turn stands over a flat square base laid diagonally on a further step.

Crosses, or parts of them, can therefore be discovered in unexpected places, evoking a real sense of the past and telling of forgotten ages. At times subsequent happenings or uses may change the name by which locals know the item, for example at Kings Caple. Here the remains of the churchyard cross has for many years been known as the Plague Cross.

When a storm destroyed the badly eroded Crosshead at Childswickham in Worcestershire it was replaced during the eighteenth century by an urn. The remainder of the cross is original.

Today the three octagonal steps and a square base to be seen in front of the church building are all that remains of the original erection that lost its relatively modern head when a falling tree destroyed it during a gale in 1947. It is reported that the original was one of very few remaining cross heads of its type, having a gabled head with a carving of Christ on a rusticated tree, his feet on the ground on one side and the seated figure of the Virgin and Child on the other.

In relatively recent times, work on the path cut through the front of the churchyard, disturbed the edge of a plague pit that was discovered near the cross. Here it was found that at least twenty-five people, and probably many more, had been buried. Since during the plague years of the seventeenth century Kings Caple had been relatively unaffected, with only a normal number of deaths recorded in the Register, this plague pit must date from the earlier pandemic of 1348 that swept through the whole of the country. Since it is likely the original cross was already standing then, it probably began to be called the Plague Cross at that time.

The outbreak during the 1600s, although not as severe as the earlier outbreak three centuries earlier, still hit parts of our area with ferocity. At Ross-on-Wye, in 1637, 315 people perished. The dead were buried at night by torchlight, still wearing their ordinary clothes and without coffins, in a pit on the north-east of the church, a cross being erected nearby as a memorial. On this is scratched a prayer for deliverance. Ross at that time was served by both a rector and vicar, and whilst the rector and richer parishioners fled to safety early in the outbreak, the vicar, John Price, stayed throughout, tending to

Although thought to have been in existence at Kings Caple prior to the outbreak of the plague in 1348, this cross also commemorates those who died during the outbreak.

The cross in the churchyard at Ross-on-Wye commemorates some 315 townsfolk who died during an outbreak of the plague in the 1600s.

the sick and administering to the dying. The church guide tells us that, 'When the plague was at its worst, he called on the dwindling survivors to join him in an act of humiliation and supplication for god's mercy and at five o'clock one morning a solemn procession moved down the High Street and past the Market Place singing the Litany'. Survivors claimed that from that day things began to get better.

During times when plague ravished the land, crosses would sometimes be erected in churchyards to enable religious services to continue in the open air, the congregation hopefully thus avoiding the spreading of the disease. The population at Treddington, Gloucestershire, is known to have suffered badly from three severe outbreaks – the first accounting for the deaths of about a quarter of the population.

Over time, the cross became the rallying point for people. Paul's Cross in London, for example, was the constant meeting place of the citizens of that city, a place where they could chat to others about any imagined or genuine miscarriages of justice. It was inevitable that they often took on a political aspect with Shire meetings or Hundred moots taking place there. Sometimes Hundreds were actually named after them, such as the Hundred of Singlecross in Sussex or Gyldecross in Norfolk.

Most punishments took place near to the church or the cross, as can be seen by the many ancient stocks, whipping posts and pillories now to be found in their vicinity. Often the last step of the cross was well worn, as this in many instances, became the seat of those in the stocks.

5

Types of Crosses

As a general rule medieval crosses bear a startling resemblance to each other, even though each has its differences.

They usually, but not always, stand on steps. These may be square, octagonal, or circular; the majority being square. They vary from the single step to tiers of up to eight, but in the main there are three; signifying the Father, Son and Holy Ghost; whilst five signify the five wounds of Christ; and eight the beatitudes mentioned in the gospel of St Matthew as a symbol of love. The steps also vary in size from quite narrow to really quite substantial blocks, the latter often being constructed of a series of blocks.

On these steps rests a socket-stone, or base, from which the shaft rises. Again these vary in size but in the majority of cases they are pretty substantial, depending on the design and content of the shaft they bear. Mostly socket-stones stand on square steps, but they give a pleasing appearance when placed on octagonal ones. As a consequence this design is taken as a model for many war memorials. Those socket-stones bearing niches will almost always be medieval, dating from the thirteenth to sixteenth centuries, so therefore may be taken to be churchyard, and not preaching, crosses although they are often so designated. These too vary in shape, design and size depending on that of the socket-stone and the purpose for which they were used. Herefordshire, having some thirty-seven of these, is extremely well-off for such niches.

The height, size and design of the shaft will also vary. In the main, the base is usually square which changes to octagonal, tapering as it rises and is mostly cut from one piece, although naturally today many of the original shafts have suffered from weathering and have been restored over the years. As has already been seen, very many of these suffered under Cromwell and were shortened and altered to serve as sundials. In some cases later restorations resulted in the complete disappearance of the shaft, being replaced by a cross as at Rendcombe in Gloucestershire and Feckenham in Worcestershire.

Originally most of these crosses would have terminated in some kind of capital or finial that supported a head of varying design. Many of these would bear sculptured figures, the majority being the figure of Christ on one side with the Virgin on the other. Or they may have a tabernacle head with panels bearing these figures with, in addition, figures of saints or clerics.

The cross at Rendcombe, Gloucestershire, received a new cross-head some hundred years ago.

Crosses are usually divided into several different types – preaching or wayside, churchyard or weeping, although in many cases the true definition of these can be muddled since there are very few that can be singularly so defined, for most will have been used for several different purposes. Indeed, there can hardly be a cross in the country where, at some time or other, preaching has not taken place, although its original erection may have been for a different purpose. There are also market crosses; those marking boundaries or set at crossroads or wells. In addition one can find sanctuary crosses, guidepost and memorial crosses, especially those commemorating well-known personages. Others mark victories or are in thanksgiving, and many of the country's war memorials are in the form of the old churchyard cross. These often use part or all of an old medieval cross.

There would seem to be great inequality of sites throughout the country as to where these are to be found – our area, along with Somerset, contains many examples whilst others have very few. In Kent, for example, there would appear to be only two, one at Folkstone and the other at Teynham although from wills of the Middle Ages it is obvious that others were positively known to have been standing. Perhaps in some cases the Cromwellian armies were more industrious or the locals, having in some cases been served ill by the monastic bodies that ruled their lives, were so relieved at their apparent release, they destroyed everything that reminded them of their servitude.

Preaching and Churchyard Crosses

It is often difficult to accurately differentiate between pure preaching crosses and those erected later as churchyard crosses, since these dominated every churchyard before the Reformation. The head of the cross usually contained a rood (a crucifix) on one side and figures of the Virgin and Child on the other, under a gabled head. Sometimes these medieval crosses would be carved with bible stores and used for ceremonial and liturgical purposes, processions being made to them at times of church festivals, such as that of Corpus Christi and Rogationtide and in particular, one held on Palm Sunday.

Whilst the observance of this service varied slightly in different places, this latter observance was a very complicated event, and seems to have originated in France, the Rhineland and the Low Countries. Having such scattered beginnings it was inevitable that the ceremony should develop along differing lines, but in most cases it would be connected with the churchyard cross and in larger towns, the town entrances and gates. As a general rule the service consisted of several sections: the Epistle and gospel, the blessing of palms, the procession to/or including the cross where probably a sermon would be preached and the return to the church. The procession itself would leave the church, the congregation carrying branches of yew, sallow or box, signifying palms, and would be preceded by a blood-red wooden cross and two banners.

At the first station the gospel was read. The bloody cross then gave way to one of silver, carried in front of the Host in a box known as the Pyx (from the Latin pyxis and Greek pyxos meaning boxtree or boxwood) and any relics the church may have had. The casket containing the Host (the wafer symbolising the sacrificed body of Christ) was used in blessing the people in certain services and also for carrying to the sick. Earlier it had been simply a box in which valuables were kept, but was adopted by Christianity as a receptacle for relics and for the sacrament. Following a Mass at the foot of the cross, the cross itself was wreathed with 'palm' branches, and a third station made at the entrance to the church where the Host and relics were held aloft above the heads of the procession, and everyone would bend their heads as they entered the building, the fourth and last station being made in front of the rood.

As we have already seen, the majority of the early crosses that are to be found at the centre of villages, or erected in distant parts of large parishes, would originally have been those set up by early Christian missionaries. They were often on or near the sites of pagan shrines and used as their base until such time as a church could be erected. Here they would preach, baptise and say Mass. Such crosses were chiefly used by the mendicant orders – Franciscan or Dominicans, both coming to this country in order to preach the gospel to the poor. The Cistercians also had the same objective when they first arrived in this country. Keeping ascetic rules and carrying with them 'preaching stools' from which they addressed their congregations, these were eventually replaced by crosses as a more convenient and dignified platform from which to address the rustics and townsfolk.

Over the years such crosses became the active centre of the community. Here proclamations and notices were announced – 'Oyez' being a corruption of the old Norman French word meaning 'Hear ye'. Here, from the foot of the cross, kings and would-be kings were proclaimed, probably at the conclusion of a Sunday-morning service, whilst during Cromwell's time, banns of marriage were published there. Vestry meetings would be held around it to discuss local grievances and wandering, usually radical, priests without a living were able to preach from it without the permission of the rector. Here too the parish clerk would notify the congregation of any newsworthy events.

It can therefore be seen that in many cases the title 'preaching cross' is something of a misnomer, for many of the crosses appearing in our churchyards probably began life as a rallying point of the people by the missionaries intent on bringing the gospel to the locals, and were not intended purely as places from which the clergy could preach. It is thought likely there remain in this area only two of the type of cross erected specifically to act as a preaching platform after the church itself had been built. These are located at Iron Acton in Gloucestershire and in Hereford where it is known as the Black Friar's Cross.

It would seem obvious that although preaching has probably taken place from all crosses, the majority were not built specifically for that purpose. However the little church at Llanveynoe in the Black Mountains has, under the church walls and opposite the cross, a stone bench at sitting height. This would seem to imply the cross was used more regularly as a spot from which to preach for there is no graveyard. This church gained a special importance in relation to the history of crosses when, in the 1920s, Mr Watkins was advised of the remains of a stone bearing a shaped cross with a groove marked down its centre, not having previously known of its existence. Investigations proved this to be a standing cross of plain monolith type, similar to those on Dartmoor, but made from local sandstone. In his book he tells us that there is a local tradition that 'St Paul came preaching over the mountains' and certainly the chief pass from Hay to Llanthony is called Bwlch-yr-Efengyl, or Gospel Pass. He continues, 'This cross stands alone in Herefordshire as being of a Celtic type'.

The cross at Iron Acton is thought to date from around 1410-19 and I cannot really do better than to quote from the excellent church guide available in the building, in attempting to describe this unusual cross, one of the most noteworthy in a county that holds a good number of various types and style of crosses. The Iron Acton cross:

> Stands on a base of three octagonal steps, the lower stage having four clustered shafts supported by light buttresses, which originally terminated in pinnacles. There was also an octagonal shaft in the centre, only the base and cap of which now remain and it is difficult to see how preaching could have been carried out satisfactorily in its original state with so limited space. From this shaft sprang fan tracery enriched with sculptured oak leaves and acorns.
>
> The upper stage is formed by a square base, on each face of which are two shields, each held by an angel with long drooping wings. Four of the shields are charged with the symbols of Our Lord's Passion… whilst two remain untouched. The base supports a four-sided shaft with cinquefoil panels, each crowned by a canopy with mouldings and finials. Above this was the shaft, which bore the cross; the original height probably being about thirty feet (9,144m). The shield bearing the arms of Acton and Fitz-Nicoll show that the builder was the first Sir Robert Poyntz, who married, as his second wife, Katherine Fitz-Nicoll. As he doesn't use his own paternal arms it must be supposed that he had for the time adapted, as was his right, the arms of the grandmother, Maud. As he died in 1439, the date of the cross must be a little earlier.

When writing of it in 1875, Pooley remarked that:

> The stone of which it is made is very hard and the carvings on it are perfect; but it has been mutilated designedly. It had evidently been destroyed by heavy missiles, there are marks on the upper part where stones have struck but whether the remaining part was too solid for further mischief or whether the inhabitants of the houses on the other side objected to the proceedings, we are not informed.

The Cross at Iron Acton is believed to be one of the few crosses actually built for the purpose of preaching.

The cross at Hereford probably dates from the time of Richard II. It was set up by the Black Friars who came to the city during the time of St Thomas Canteloup and were given land outside the Widemarsh Gate of the city at around 1246, by order of Sir John Daniel who was later beheaded for interference in the baronial wars in the reign of Edward III. In this country members of this order were often known as Black Friars due to the black mantle they wore over their white habits. They were also known as 'Friars Preachers', regularly giving sermons to the local populace from special preaching crosses, in several cases being forbidden to preach in churches by the parish priests who were jealous of the popularity achieved by the friars.

In many ways the cross here resembles that of Iron Acton, although it is hexagonal instead of square. It was set up in the churchyard of the monastery of Dominican Friars specifically for preaching, and is one of very few still remaining in the country. Standing on four steps, it has an open balustrade and a central pillar with a stone bench around it. From this pillar a cross rises above and a vaulted roof springs from six little shafts. It is thought that around the pulpit there were cloisters where the public could shelter in bad weather whilst still being able to hear the preacher. The monastery was dissolved in 1538 by Henry VIII.

The ancient cross shares the attractive rose garden with what remains of the monastic buildings. The early decorated gothic building was founded around 1276 when the church was consecrated in the presence of Edward III and his son the Black Prince and three archbishops. The church with a spire was located on the south-west of the building. The remains now standing are the refectory and friar's house of around 1322. Following the Dissolution, the site subsequently passed through inheritance to the wife of Sir Thomas Coningsby of Hampton Court, Dinmore in the north of Herefordshire, who converted one wing of the cloisters into a splendid town residence in the seventeenth century.

Blackfriar's Cross, Hereford, the only other cross in the country thought to have been built as a purely preaching cross.

However, the new house was badly damaged during the Civil War and later became a farm building.

Some preaching crosses gained an importance completely outside their original usage. One of the most celebrated of these is Paul's Cross in London where the Bishop of Exeter preached in 1461. Some time later Dr Shaw, feeling that the young Prince Edward V had no legal right to the crown, preached against his validity. Later still Charles I went in state to the same spot in order to listen to Laud preaching.

At Eckington in Worcestershire an ancient cross, said to have been a preaching cross, stands at a crossroads in the centre of the village. Its base stands on two steps, paddling in flowers. From this rises the shaft, of which about 3ft is original. Keeping it company is a war memorial dedicated on 18 April 1920. In 1897, the year of the Queen Victoria's Diamond Jubilee, the Worcestershire Archaeological Society restored the cross that had by then been used as a signpost and had deteriorated badly. Deciding to preserve intact the original remains, they completed the shaft and added a modern head.

As no evidence has been discovered of the existence of any church in the village during Saxon times, it is thought the original village cross could have been erected by monks from Pershore as a centre for public worship. Mr A.W. Fletcher in his book *Eckington, the Story of a Worcestershire Parish* tells us that the first mention of a cross does not occur until the Lay Subsidy Roll of 1327 gives the names and amounts to be paid by those taxed during the war with the Scots, mentioning an entry of 'Jahannes atte Croys'.

He also tells us that the cross was moved to its present position from the south side of the parish, adding that Trattinton, in the early nineteenth century, speaks of 'the remains of a cross near the Cross Road leading from Woolashull to Strensham Mill, on the R' Hand in a field of about 20 acres belonging to Mrs Osborne' which Mr Fletcher thinks

The Wayside Cross at Eckington, Worcestershire.

to be the field known as Saunders Place, which was assigned to Elizabeth Osborne by the Enclosure Award of 1813.

A further cross, said to be an ancient preaching cross, is to be found in the churchyard of St Michael & All Angels at Knighton-on-Teme in Worcestershire. In fact, in spite of its name, it would appear to have been one of those with far more relevance during the Easter celebrations, for in its base can be seen the niche where the Sacred Host would be deposited. The cross, thought to be far older than the church, is accompanied by an ancient yew tree, some 1,300 years of age, from where other yews can also be seen. These are thought perhaps to have been markers by which preachers were able to find their way from one preaching point to the next.

The cross stands on three steps and a square base from which part of the original shaft points. Mrs Pearl G. Davies, in her book *Knighton-above-the-Teme*, tells us that the bottom and second step were repaired in 1967 at a cost of £100. Mrs Davies is presently attempting to raise funds in order to conserve the cross that is now in need of restoration, having donated a sum in memory of her husband who died in 2004. Unfortunately, agreement for such work has taken many long months, with costs continually rising, but it is hoped work will commence before too much longer.

Another preaching cross can be found in the churchyard of St Andrew's Church at Hampton, near Evesham. Originally situated on four or five fifteenth-century steps, two of which remain, it has an octagonal carved socket-stone from which rises a modern shaft. The tabernacle top is very eroded, but is believed to have had a quatrefoil or flower decoration on three sides whilst the fourth held a seated abbot. Since Hampton would have been *en route* between Evesham and Tewkesbury, this church could well have been the first stop for abbots travelling that way.

What has been known locally for many years as a preaching cross is one at Wick near Pershore in Worcestershire. However, from his research Mr Laurie Clifton Crick feels this to be one of those misnomers, since although the base and shaft are certainly ancient, the cross was probably not erected until after the church had been built. It is sometimes thought that it was transported to its present site in recent times, bearing in mind there wasn't even any consecrated or fenced churchyard at Wick until a piece of land was purchased for the purpose in 1877, but it does appear in its current position on a map of 1849. The land was obtained from Charles Smith Hudson following the formation of the Pershore Burial Board in 1874, which the inhabitants of Wick did not wish to join. It therefore seems likely that the cross remained on the spot where it had always been.

The cross at Knighton-on-Teme, Herefordshire, which is thought to be older than the church.

The cross at Hampton, near Evesham, Worcestershire.

The cross in the small village of Wick, Worcestershire, that was restored in 1912.

By the end of the 1800s the shifting of the line of the road and the formal enclosure of the new burial ground had left the cross marooned in a sheep field, where it fell into further disrepair. It was thanks to Reverend Charles Henry Bickerton Hudson, who resided opposite at Upper Wick House, that restoration took place. He instructed G.F. Bodley, who had previously erected the lych-gate to the church in 1899, to undertake its restoration. This saw an inscription cut into the stone of the four sides of the base and a heavy new head with ornate canopied niches and figures. In 1984 this head fell during a period of high winds. Until this new top was added the cross was described variously as 'a tapering octagonal shaft' and 'a slender shaft' with no reference to any actual cross or upper decoration.

The restoration work was carried out by R. Bridgeman & Sons of Lichfield, the workmen placing coins and other objects of the time beneath the base of the cross. The finished cross was blessed at a special service on 27 September 1911 at which Reverend Canon Knox-Little of Worcester was the visiting preacher. Hymns were sung in procession to the cross, and the Vicar of Wick, Reverend John Jervis, said special prayers at the site. Following the recent loss of the heavy head, a village fund was set up and the cross was repaired minus any head.

It can therefore be seen that several of the so-called preaching crosses to be found in churchyards could well have been erected for other purposes, although a church guide for St Mary Magdelene at Twyning in Worcestershire says it is thought that very little actual preaching took place inside churches until the post-medieval period.

However, during the medieval period the churchyard itself could be an extremely busy place where, on religious feast days, there would be dancing, games and perhaps a fair, which travelling merchants attended. Such fairs were primarily concerned with trade, attracting traders from afar and also itinerant entertainers. However, subsequent economic and social change eventually displaced the commercial element, leaving the travelling showmen to perpetuate the event, which could become very unruly especially as centuries passed.

The fair in Pershore was originally established by Royal Grant. Towards the end of the tenth century the secular canons were displaced by Benedictine monks, who dedicated the abbey to Saints Mary and Eadburga, the daughter of King Edward. Eadburga had always shown a predilection for the religious life and entered a convent, where she lived until her death. She was buried at Winchester. Later, some of her bones were sent to Pershore where they were treasured as relics, seemingly having a miraculous power in healing the sick. Such relics were usually kept in abbeys and attracted pilgrims from afar, their pious offerings adding greatly to the abbey's revenues. Being short of money, the Abbot of Pershore applied to King Henry III for assistance and was granted a patent to hold a public Annual Fair upon St Eadburga's Feast Day, this privilege being confirmed by succeeding monarchs.

Over the centuries the fair degenerated so far that local worthies determined to rid forever the disgraceful scenes occurring in the churchyards where the fair was mainly held. In 1831 an article appeared in *The Worcestershire Mirror* denouncing the fair as:

Degrading to human nature those disgraceful amusements which come under the denomination of Pershore Fair... Scarcely was the Sabbath worship concluded last Sunday when the sacred gates were thrown open and the churchyard filled with the very scum of society, who, regardless of that solemnity in the heart of every Christian... began erecting booths, stalls and stages for the ensuing Fair.

It continues, saying that on approaching the churchyard the writer:

Was greeted with all the noise and bustle of a country fair, a large caravan of wild beasts in one part, giants and dwarfs in another, and stages of dancing girls resting upon the scattered graves endeavouring to out-bawl each other, giving utterances to low and filthy jests and stunning every spectator with a discord of grating instruments.

In other parts were stalls selling various items whilst tombstones were converted into the backs of bowling alleys.

Disquiet regarding this event eventually came to a head in 1830 when the churchyard gates were barricaded to keep the showmen out, with stalwart local men attempting to protect their graveyard. But their efforts were to no avail, the showmen using an elephant to drag open the gates. In order to evict the fair from the churchyards an alternative site had to be found for the revels. By 1936 public subscription had raised £3,000, enabling six houses at the end of Broad Street to be demolished, creating a large square. It had also been possible to purchase, for £650, the Fair Rights from the Earl of Harewood, the then owner. By offering toll-free space to those manning the fair, a change of site was possible.

Crosses were also erected during medieval times as a memorial to those gone before. At a time when graves were not marked and there was no central point to which folk could gather to remember and mourn their loved ones, a communal cross would be erected for this purpose. The majority of these churchyard crosses were erected on the south side of the church building, which would be in accordance with the general prejudice against being buried on the north side. Exceptions to this rule can be found at Wigmore, Hampton Bishop, Hentland, Fownhope and Foy in Herefordshire, where the crosses are on the north side. Also in Herefordshire, at Ballingham old church the cross is on the east and at Aymestrey and Dorstone on the western side.

It is obvious, therefore, that many churchyard crosses were erected purely to act as a communal cross, and it is supposed that one such example is the cross to be found at North Cerney, Gloucestershire. Restored relatively recently, this fourteenth-century cross was originally erected as a memorial for all buried on the south side of the church, and now serves as the village's war memorial.

Fear of being buried on the north side of the church continued for many years, and it was not until relatively recently that burials took place here, especially following the custom of erecting individual stones, which came into practice during the seventeenth century. As in many other places, the coffin was taken out through the north door, as it still is at North Cerney, it being the only time this door is used. In a great number of churches the original north doors have been blocked. The cross here is set on three square slabs, the lower being the deepest. The socket-stone is concave in its upper bed and square above, with truncated angles. From this rises a tapering shaft culminating in a Celtic cross. This head was missing in Pooley's time, although he did wonder if this would be found in an adjacent wall.

The church itself is well worth a visit, with its round, richly carved pillars, Jacobean low oak panelling, a really old pulpit and a magnificent rood loft re-erected as a war memorial. Steps built into the side of the chancel arch allow access onto the loft where I found, carved in the corner stones, a jolly looking little monkey.

Thus the origins of many of the crosses found in churchyards are lost in the mists of time. For example, when in Medieval times new erections or graves came to be built near an earlier cross, the original could be undermined and so were replaced, and usually placed at the south side of the church facing east. In most cases, the carving and ornamentation of the new cross would follow the style of architecture prevalent at the time they were re-erected, not always following the original design.

The cross at North Cerney thought to have been erected as a communal one to enable folk to remember their loved ones in the days prior to the erection of individual gravestones.

During the eighteenth century, several crosses came to be enclosed by metal railings that would seem to be acting against the original idea that such erections be for community use. It was therefore probably a good thing that many such railings were taken away to assist with the war effort during the Second World War, but unfortunately much of greater use also disappeared at the same time. You win some and you lose some!

Wayside Crosses

In addition to early preaching crosses, many were set up along roadsides in villages or at a point where roads met. A paper printed at Westminster in 1496 says crosses were put there so that 'when folk passed they should give thanks to Him that died on the cross and worship Him above all things.' Along pilgrim ways there were obviously many, although as a number of these were built in out-of-the-way spots they often came to be used for other purposes. Fortunately in more recent times several of these crosses have been rescued and restored.

The cross at Ripple stands amongst houses in the centre of the village and is thought to have been raised for this purpose since it stands at the spot where two ancient tracks meet, traces of which can still be seen. The cross stands on three steps and a square base, its tall shaft capped by a small point, and is protected by iron railings on a long established grassy patch. The remains of a further cross can also be found in the churchyard itself. Springing from a square, chamfered topped socket-stone on three steps, part of the shaft still exists, which, in the more recent past has been turned into a sundial.

The cross at Ripple, Worcestershire, stands where two ancient tracks meet.

Several villages have wayside or village crosses that were probably set up as preaching crosses. But over time these became the point where tolls were collected and tithes paid, thus gaining additional importance. One village cross can be seen at Ashelworth, Gloucestershire. This consists of a 10ft-high octagonal shaft let into a square socket-stone with a bevelled top and two square steps. The shaft is topped by a lantern head with four niches sheltering different scenes. One shows a crucifixion scene (rood) with St John holding a book and Mary a box. On the opposite side, not so well preserved, is shown the Virgin and Child together with a kneeling woman.

Of the two other sculptures, each containing figures, one is so disfigured it is impossible to tell whom it represents but it is thought it could be Robert Fitzharding, the original donor who ended his life as a canon of the monastery he had founded and who died in 1170. The other more clearly shows an apostolic figure carrying a book at whose feet there is a kneeling person with what appears to be a sheep's head. It is believed that this figure probably represents St Augustine, the patron of the abbey that held Ashelworth. He had been specially directed to convert the Anglo-Saxons to Christianity. In this he was very successful, in fact it is said that on one day he baptised some 10,000 folk of both sexes in the River Swale. He is also known to have baptised Ethelbert, the pagan king of Kent. Pooley though, wonders if the artist who designed the sculpture may have muddled St Augustine, the prior of the convent, with St Augustine, Bishop of Hippo, to whom the abbey was dedicated.

The cross, resting on a chamfered square base and two square steps has a somewhat chequered history in that until 1970 it was to be found in two different places – the steps and base being on the village green whilst the head was in the churchyard. The latter was discovered in the nineteenth century, hidden in the hearth of one of the cottages on the green. It was reunited through the generosity of a local farmer and landowner, the late Mr Jack Chamberlayne.

Head of Ashleworth Cross

Ashelworth, Gloucestershire, where parts of the cross were to be found in the churchyard, with the steps and base on the village green.

Close-up of the head of Ashelworth Cross. (Reproduced courtesy of Dr Jeremy Barnes)

Weeping Crosses

In addition to those crosses used in connection with the Easter ceremonies the name could also be applied to other types. At the time that many of the churchyard crosses were erected, miscreants were expected to do penance as punishment for their wrongdoing. On confessing to the priest, they would be instructed to undertake some humbling form of penitence. Rimmer thinks the cross at Ampney Crucis may well be a weeping cross. Penance often took the form of being told to attend at a particular cross 'in order to weep over delinquencies and whilst there to loudly declare them to any passers by'. Often such instructions entailed doing so barefooted or on one's knees. An old proverb states, 'The way to heaven is by Weeping Crosses', whilst another old saying states, 'He that goeth out with often loss, at last comes home by Weeping Cross'.

Often there were hollows in the base of crosses and at one time it was thought these could be knee-holes in which penitents could kneel to pray, but it is now believed they were intended for votive offerings. It is not easy therefore to spot which of the crosses bearing niches were intended to receive offerings, which to hold Holy Water or which to hold the Pyx.

Weeping crosses were, however, not always used for penitential observances. At Shrewsbury on the feast of Corpus Christi, groups from various guilds would congregate to offer prayers for a good harvest. Sometimes such crosses were also set up as a mark of private grief. Thus at Caen one was erected to Matilda, Queen of William the Conqueror, considered by many to have been treated in an unfair and cruel manner.

It was also the custom to erect what came to be known as weeping crosses along roads leading to old parish churches, for the convenience of funerals. On occasion coffins needed to be carried long distances and as there were then no hearses, this was often a difficult undertaking. With roads bad and bodies heavy, resting places were needed along the way, with crosses often being erected at such places. At each, a prayer for the soul of the departed was offered and sometimes the 'de profundis' sung, the mourners being comforted as they passed along the long sad road with their dear ones for the last time. Such crosses were sometimes therefore known as 'cortege crosses'.

There are several cases where crosses were set up marking each stage of the several-mile journey where a body rested, the idea probably just an extension of the lych-gate system where it was usual for the corpse to rest before being carried into the church for the funeral service. In France along the road from Paris to St Denys, the last resting place of many French Kings, crosses were erected almost every few hundred yards but all of these were swept away during the Revolution.

William of Malmesbury tells in his chronicle of the procession that accompanied Aldhelm, a celebrated Saxon Saint, who died fifty miles from the Abbey of Glastonbury where he was to be buried. We are told that in William's day there were seven crosses still remaining, known as 'bishop stones'. It is reported that at these crosses the sick were cured.

Perhaps the most well known of this type of cross are the Eleanor crosses. Although not in our area, these crosses are so important in the history of the cross, I feel it is important to mention them here. In 1255, when she was ten years old, Eleanor of Spain was betrothed to Edward I, who was aged fifteen. She remained in France until she was twenty, when she joined Edward, where they lived mainly at Windsor castle. Sadly, of their fifteen children only six survived. Their marriage was a true love match, the queen accompanying Edward everywhere, helping him in every way and she was much loved by the people.

She was on her way to join Edward in his Scottish wars, when she became ill. Edward immediately came south but she was dead before he reached her. Eleanor died at Harby in Nottinghamshire on 18 November 1291, at the home of one Richard Weston, of which all traces have since disappeared. A cross was erected at every resting place of her funeral procession on its way to Westminster.

Eleanor's body probably rested in fifteen places but it is believed only twelve crosses were erected. The distance from Harby to Westminster by the old roads was 159 miles – thirteen and a half probably being travelled each day since roads in the east of England were particularly bad, especially in winter. It is believed the sites of the crosses were Lincoln, Grantham, Stamford, Geddington, Northampton, Stoney-Stratford, Woburn, Dunstable, St Albans, Waltham, West Cheap and Charing. The Queen's heart was deposited in the church of the Friars Praedicants (or Preaching Friars) in London and her bowels in the chapel of the Virgin in Lincoln Cathedral where there is a statue to her and another to her husband.

The procession set out on 4 December and arrived on 17 December. After leaving Stamford, the normal route was abandoned to enable some of the religious houses to be visited *en route* and it seems that after St Albans, the King left the procession in order to meet it when it entered the city of London.

It is sad that all but three of the Eleanor crosses have disappeared, leaving only those at Geddington, Northampton and Waltham. Edward, a great soldier and politician, could little have dreamed that the beautiful memorials he erected attesting to his great love for his wife would be destroyed by a later age. He must have thought these structures with no central shaft – resulting in a firmer, stronger interior – would last forever. In fact, the remains of those crosses left standing show how graceful and beautiful they all must have been.

Geddington stands north-east of Kettering in Northamptonshire, and today it is a small village. However, in the past it possessed a royal palace, where weighty affairs of State were often deliberated, and it was here that Henry II decided on his expedition to the Holy Land. The cross is very Spanish in appearance and is thought to be the work of one of Eleanor's own countrymen. Standing on eight steps, the shaft reaches loftily to the skies, a series of niches holding sculpted figures, before continuing more narrowly and culminating in pinnacles. From an old print published in 1788 it seems there was a third story, used as a sundial. Triangular in design, it is slightly off-centre, eight diaper patterns covering the whole of the lower stage, and the cross is erected over a spring of clear water that never runs dry. Wells and crosses are often found together, again harking back to the old pagan religion adapted by early Christian missionaries.

From Geddington the cortege went to Hardingstone on the outskirts of Northampton where it arrived on 9 December. Today, it stands about a mile from the centre of the town, resting on a grassy mound on a busy road that runs alongside the wall of Delapie Park, the seat of the Bouverie family. It is octagonal, with the top of the cross broken, but the shaft probably ended in pierced gables with pinnacles between, from which the cross proper began.

The cross at Waltham in Hertfordshire, the last resting place of the body before entering London, was at risk from traffic as long ago as the early 1720s when the Revernd Stukeley attempted to save it. In spite of two extensive nineteenth-century restorations, by 1988 it was in a very sorry state, with protective railings having been smashed. However, thanks to the Hertfordshire County Council it was restored and a pedestrian precinct created

The remains of the Eleanor cross at Northampton and that at Geddington.

around it. This cross has been copied exactly in that which commemorates the Crimean War at Westminster.

It is probable that on entering London the body of Eleanor would have rested for the night in St Paul's before being taken to the village of Charing, the last place where it rested before being buried in Westminster Abbey. This event gave its name to the locality, the cross having been erected for the 'beloved queen'. It is said Charing is a corruption of the words, 'Chere Reine', meaning dear or beloved queen. However, it is now thought the area was called Cyrringe since well before the date of the cross, the name referring to the old English word meaning a bend, either on the Roman road to the west, or to a bend in the River Thames. The cross that now stands in front of Charing Cross station is a copy of the original.

Market Crosses

Market crosses originated in towns near monastic establishments and formed a central point where the order would have sent a monk or prior on market days to preach to those attending there. The attendees would have ranged from merchants and craftsmen to ordinary folk selling surplus fruit and vegetables and those interested only in obtaining a few additional pennies in order to ensure the survival of their families. The monks would also collect the tithes due from their farmers and flocks and collect tolls paid by both farmers and dealers in country produce, for the privilege of selling within the limits of the town. At this time such tolls would have been strictly under the control of the local abbey, the monks also influencing the daily life of the town. In some cases this right to collect a tax from farmers for each head of cattle brought into the town for sale later passed to influential families in the area and continued for some centuries. In addition to those selling and purchasing, others would congregate; entertainers ranging from professional actors, musicians and dancers to folk displaying curiosities and freaks. Markets would also hold more than their fair share of whores, thieves and pickpockets.

Market centres quickly became active meeting places and a rallying point for the local inhabitants. However, over the centuries what began as an institution for the betterment of the population often degenerated into a purely materialistic one, as we have seen occurred at Pershore. In spite of the loss of the religious aspect of the event, market days and fairs were eagerly looked forward to by the local populace as a day of entertainment and enjoyment, one where it would be possible to meet friends and catch up on the latest news and scandals. As time passed additional markets came into being, such as those held for specific reasons, for example for the selling of animals, or for times when servants could be hired. By the middle of the 1800s there were two such markets held in Pershore – one on the Wednesday before and another after 11 October, the second Wednesday being a 'Runaway Fair' at which labourers who had left a job obtained at the first fair, sought alternative employment.

In medieval times any village more than six miles from a market was entitled to apply to the Crown for one of their own – if this was granted a cross would often be erected to mark the site. But in many cases a market cross would have started life as a simple preaching cross – a tall shaft on steps – perhaps later becoming more elaborate, some having niches for sculptured figures and intricate moulding or carving. Some market crosses, particularly those in villages, are quite simple affairs whilst others, especially those in towns, are more elaborate, such as the crosses at Chichester, Salisbury and Malmesbury.

As time passed it was felt necessary to erect some kind of cover to shield folk from the worst of the weather, so a kind of house was erected. The early coverings probably only offered partial shelter but around the cross booths would have been erected if necessary. These structures would sometimes enclose the original cross, its head appearing above the roof. Thus it is possible to see where an original cross has been protected in this way, for obviously if the cross appears through the roof of the building, the covering, or roof, must have been erected subsequently to the cross itself.

There are only a few of these covered-in market crosses remaining throughout the country, those that do so being found mainly in the north. One of the reasons for this is that the early canopies were made of oak and later used in other buildings. Market houses often followed an octagonal design, although varying in style and name depending on the part of the country and the period when they were erected. For example, that at Winchester is called the 'Butter Cross' whilst that at Salisbury is known as the 'Poultry Cross'. Some of the early market crosses, such as those at Gloucester, Coventry and Abingdon, had little turrets with vanes called girouettes. They revolved with the wind, and the gilt covering glittered in the sun.

As far as I've been able to ascertain there are none of these old covered market crosses to be found in the area in which we are interested, although at Ross the marketplace contained a high cross in the sixteenth century with a boothall attached to houses in Underhill and jutting into the street. Here, market tolls were collected. The medieval market place was much larger than the present area and by the thirteenth century the market stalls had become purely a row of shops and houses. In the seventeenth century this boothall was deemed to be unsatisfactory, so much so that local resident Thomas Webbe left money in his will to replace it. Nothing was actually done, however. Although local tradition has, for many years, held that the present market house was built by Frances, wife of the 2nd Duke of Somerset and Lady of the Manor at around 1670, it appears from later research the old boothall was demolished sometime in the 1850s, along with seven houses adjacent to it, when the present market house was built. This new building of soft red sandstone, which is divided into two gables, is open on each side and occupied more space than the original building. However, it would appear that the high cross disappeared at this time.

The original octagonal form of the building became quadrangular with a hall over the market. Originally designed to be used as the magistrate's court, taxation office and market office it has, during its 300-year history also been a school room, welfare office, dance hall, and more recently, the town library. It has been used for all major occasions in the town, seeing proclamations and announcements made from its steps that were also used by preachers for ecumenical church services. Not only has the building seen great changes in the town, it has itself undergone a number of changes, including the removal of stairs outside the main structure that must have led to a door at first-floor level facing down Broad Street. This door was later used as a balcony for civic proclamations. The internal heavy oak staircase must have been added after 1690 with the upper room being used as a courtroom by manor officials.

On the closure of the library, consultations began in 1992 in order to decide how best to use the building once it had been repaired and refurbished. It was decided to create a

A postcard, dated 1913, showing the Market House at Ross.

museum and a centre to encourage local crafts and skills. By 1997 the very popular heritage centre opened on the site, which continues to grow in strength.

By the sixteenth and seventeenth centuries market halls had become the symbols of the status of a town and that at Leominster was especially fine, principally due to its top quality wool trade. The market hall was built on the site of a previous one at the top of Broad Street. Here, guild meetings were held in the upper part. There were nine master trade guilds in Leominster who also had additional civic responsibilities, such as keeping various town buildings in repair. By the early 1790s complaints were being made that the market hall was causing traffic problems and in 1853 the town obtained an Act of Parliament permitting its demolition and the building of a new one.

This old building was auctioned and sold, the grandson of the famous inventor and mill owner Richard Arkwright hoping to resurrect it as a library and museum. The building having been dismantled, it was later re-erected as a private house. A new roof and masonry ground floor was added behind the columns to make more living space and help to stabilise the structure. In 1928 it was again put on the market, the prospective purchaser being the American William Randolph Hurst who wanted to remove the building to the South Wales coast. However, the borough council obtained a preservation order on the building and purchased it, converting it into offices with a Mayor's parlour and reception area on the ground floor.

We have already seen how the market hall at Pembridge evolved from an early waymark stone to a completed market hall and there are several other impressive market houses in the area, in particular those at Ledbury, Dursley and Ross. We know that the house at Dursley was erected on the site of a butter cross that, by the time it was built in 1738, had become a 'ruinous arcade'. The town has market charters from Edward IV and

The Market House at Leominster, now in use as offices of the borough council.

Henry VIII so must have been a small but thriving centre during medieval times. The market house here (incorporating the town hall) was built in 1738, its upper storey resting on twelve arches. At its end is a statue of Queen Anne. She had been instrumental in assisting the rebuilding of the church tower following its collapse in 1699, so was held in great affection locally. Thus, twenty-four years after her death, this statue commemorates her support. On the side of the building is a carved coat of arms of the Escourt family who were Lords of the Manor.

At Ledbury the market house is an attractive 'black & white' building erected on wooden stilts and standing in the centre of the town. The market itself had been long established when, in the late sixteenth century, a local trader suggested the building of a permanent market house on the site where two ramshackle rows of shops remained. With the assistance of subscriptions from the public he purchased Shoppe Row for about £40 and demolished it. Work on the proposed new building commenced in 1617 to a design allowing the main building to be raised on sixteen stilts. This allowed for small shops to be established beneath the main construction that would have had a timber frame and brick infill.

It is thought the building was designed by architect John Abel who is known to have built the market hall at Leominster, although there is little evidence to support the theory. It took some fifty years before the building was completed as it stands today, and it is probable the design may have been changed over time. When John Phillips died in 1655 there was no money available to complete the work but the trustees, by taking £40 from two legacies left for the provision of clothes for poor people, were able to eventually complete the work in 1688, having agreed in writing that twelve poor people a year would receive clothing purchased from profits from the market house. The upper rooms of market houses

A postcard, postmarked 1906, showing the Market House at Dursley.

The seventeenth-century market house at Ledbury, Gloucestershire.

built to such a design were often used for storage, for the transaction of business or for use as a town hall, but today the building is mainly used for meetings, sales and exhibitions.

Near the church at the west end of the market place at Cirencester stands the original market cross, a high cross being located here in 1927 following a series of moves since the eighteenth century. This was referred to in a document of 1413 as being the 'Nova Crux', which would seem to imply there had been a predecessor. Of six crosses described by Pooley in 1868 this is the only one that survives. Originally opposite the Ram Inn at the western end of the market place, it was described by Rudder in 1800, as standing 'on a base 10ft square, with four steps on each side, with an octagonal column or pillar supporting a capital which was much defaced'. In 1795 the cross was moved to Cirencester Park, to a plantation known as Cathedral Firs in the northern sector of Oakley Wood, and having stood there for some years it was again moved to a spot near the woodhouse.

Of the other five, both Fuller in 1932 and Slater in 1976 state that the Pig Cross stood at the northern end of Dyer Street opposite the Waterloo Passage where the pig market was held. In 1800 Rudder recalled a sundial fixed on a pillar at this spot that had been taken down before 1795, whilst 'Site of Cross' is recorded on the 1875 Ordnance Survey of the town. In 1800 the round pedestal of the Dyer Street or London Road Cross is described as standing 'near the extremity of the borough at the first station of water at the end of Dyer Street'. Rudder also records the existence of a churchyard cross in the parish churchyard but states 'it was not entire within living memory', whilst the round pedestal of the cross that stood at the junction of Tetbury Road, Park Lane and Castle Street was 'still remembered' although 'removed'. The sixth cross stood at the junction of Querns Lane and Cricklade Street and marked the bounds of the township, as did those crosses at Sheep Street and London Road. It is not known exactly why these demolished crosses were originally erected, although obviously at least one was a boundary cross and another a churchyard cross.

At Stow-on-the-Wold there is a true market cross standing in the centre of the town in what would originally have been a much larger market square. This was thought to have been erected in the 1400s by the Chesters, a wealthy and important local family who also founded a chantry in the church and built the church tower. The cross stands on three square steps with a square to octagonal socket-stone from which rises a broached octagonal shaft, some 7ft high. This is topped by a tabernacle finial and the four sides have carved panels dedicated to events and people who were of importance to the town, namely the Civil War, the crucifixion, Edward the Confessor and the wool trade. The latter was particularly important as it formed the basis for the prosperity of the town. Panels on the cross tell us it has been restored on two occasions, the first in 1878 in memory of James

The Old Market Cross is the only remaining example of several crosses that once stood at Cirencester.

The Market Cross at Stow-on-the-Wold is thought to have been erected in the 1400s.

Chamberlayne, a local dignitary, and the second in 1995. In Pooley's time the cross had a shaft chiselled into it to take a pipe – allowing it to be used as a street lamp.

At Chipping Sodbury in Gloucestershire there is known to have been a market cross dating from around 1370 which was replaced in 1522. There was a cattle market in the main street in 1837 that ceased in 1954 due to health regulations. Pooley tells us that in his time there was a cross in a garden belonging to the Catholic chapel, said to have been moved there by Reverend R.M. Cooper in 1862, he having purchased it from a Mr Clark. The cross is described as having a tapering octagonal shaft of two stones cemented together that could originally have been a monolith, the socket below being unusually large with hollowed square sides and raised on modern masonry. This had apparently been brought there from near the Portcullis Inn by a Mr Parker, a bailiff, to the orchard over the brook near Trotman's Mill in an attempt to preserve it from further dilapidation. This was especially important due to the increase in public traffic. Part of the early cross is said to be incorporated into today's 1919 war memorial that faces up the long, wide main street.

Due to their original function, one of the uses to which market crosses were used was to inculcate the sacredness of bargains. In Middleham in Yorkshire there is a platform on which are two further platforms, one carrying an effigy of an animal, the other suppos-edly representing a cheese. Here the farmers would walk up the opposing flights of steps when concluding a bargain, shaking hands over the sculptures.

A fine example of a cross that could be placed under the heading of either church-yard or market is to be found in the churchyard of St Leonard's Church at Tortworth in

Tortworth, Gloucestershire.
The Market Cross is thought to be
that of Sir Nicholas Kyngeston.

Gloucestershire, since this fourteenth-century cross, with its modern top, is thought to be the market cross of Sir Nicholas de Kyngeston. As Lord of the Manor he had purchased the Right of Market and Fair in 1304 and as such the cross became the focal point both of the church and the village.

In contrast crosses built purely as a religious symbol were sometimes utilised by the populace as a centre for market use, sellers making use of the steps on which to sit in order to sell their produce. It is believed this was the case at Much Marcle and probably at Madley whilst it is known regular markets took place at the cross in Bodenham (all in Herefordshire).

Boundary and Sanctuary Crosses

When Constantine, the first Christian Emperor, ordered crosses to be erected to replace pagan emblems, they also acted as terminals marking off different lands and ownerships. Such boundary crosses were used in the same way during Saxon times and the early Middle Ages. References in old charters refer to various boundary crosses that are variously described as being 'a gilded cross', a 'wooden cross', a 'stone cross', or a 'red cross', even sometimes as a 'Christ Symbol'. These usually served to mark the limits of church property. The monks at Edmundsbury erected four crosses, one at each extremity of the town to define the limits of their authority, whilst Bishop Losinga raised a cross at Norwich to serve as a boundary mark between the land of the church and the borough. St Guthlac also set up a cross at Croyland for the same purpose. Occasionally boundary crosses would also mark the spot beyond which wrongdoers could obtain sanctuary.

An Irish canon of the eighth century directed that a cross be set up on all consecrated ground, not only to mark the bounds but also to sanctify the spot. However this decision later rebounded on the church. As church property was exempt from taxation, unauthorised crosses began to be erected until it was necessary to pass a law a few centuries later forbidding men to set up a cross falsely. It was at this time that Rogation processions began, when the clergy laid earth and grass upon the boundary stones, both to mark the boundaries and to offer prayers to avert pestilence.

It was also at a boundary cross that friends of medieval pilgrims would gather to wish them 'God speed', particularly if the pilgrim was a member of a guild. Preparing for his journey at one of the shrines, either in this country or overseas, he would be sent on his way with prayers, especially if his destination was one of the well-known pilgrimage sites. Thus it was that in the 'Gild of Resurrection' in Lincoln it was ordained that, 'If any brother or sister wishes to make the pilgrimage to Rome, St James of Galicia or the Holy Land, he shall forewarn the Gild, and all the brethren and sisters shall go with him and each shall give him a half-penny at the least'. The same rule is found in the Gild of the Fullers at Lincoln founded in 1297 when a pilgrim going to Rome would be accompanied as far as the Queen's Cross outside the town providing he left on a Sunday or a feast day.

Whilst in medieval times crosses marked boundaries of ecclesiastical properties, county boundaries were also often marked by crosses and meare stones. In Oldham there were seven crosses to mark the estate owned by the Hospital of St John of Jerusalem. These boundary crosses are usually quite plain and relatively short in stature.

Crosses were also often erected where roads met and many travellers passed by. There pilgrims would kneel to ask for aid for their journey and protection from outlaws, accidents and sudden death. A cross would also often be set up at wells and springs in an attempt to wean newly converted Christians from superstitious thoughts and pagan customs, whilst continuing the idea of the sacredness of springs. Many of these markers were painted white, their remains today hidden away in corners of old paths or ditches that could well have served as roads in the past. These crosses could have been erected by the White Cross Knights of Malta or those of St John of Jerusalem, or may have been the work of the Carmelites (the White Friars).

In the centre of the village of Condicote in Gloucestershire is a walled grassy circle that could once have been the village green as the village pump was erected there. Nearby is an ancient cross set on a square base and two fourteenth-century steps. The base bears inscriptions which are now almost illegible. On the east face is inscribed, 'To every-one that thirsteth come ye to the waters'. On the west side it says, 'Restored 1862. W.B. Van Notten Pole, Rector', whilst the north face reads, 'This well is reserved for the domestic purposes of the inhabitants of this parish, for all other uses recourse to the pump and trough is respectfully suggested. See resolution of vestry, March 16th, 1865.' This cross is sited above a spring of water and it appears that Reverend Van Notten Pole also added the present shaft, some 6ft tall, to an existing base, topping it with an ornamental cross as a finial.

It is thought by some that such crosses could also have served as signposts – certainly in the distant past such posts, sometimes with god's heads on them, were erected at cross roads to point the way and many of these could have been replaced later replaced by a Christian symbol. It is known that many of these were whitewashed or plastered, but it is uncertain whether this was in order to make them more prominent. It is known that at one time the the the exterior of St Alban's Abbey Church, and also the White Castle in Wales,

The village cross of Condicote, Gloucestershire, built over a spring.

were coated with whitewash from top to base. Such practice would certainly have made it easier to spot signs painted in this way, both during the day as well as at night.

In Cheshire, in the wild region of the Delamere Forest, there are several ancient crosses erected for the convenience of travellers. Once under the shadow of such an erection they would be safe from robbery and violence at the hands of outlaws, since as a general rule the sanctity of the cross was adhered to. This protected fugitives from violence as long as they kept within bounds.

Under an ecclesiastical law endowed by King Athelstan in the year 900, and not abolished until 1623, fugitives from justice could, upon reaching a stone chair known as a frithstoll (from the Anglo-Saxon *frith* or *frid* meaning peace) claim refuge and immunity for a certain length of time. Originally, this privilege, known as the Right of Sanctuary, was only around a bishop's throne and therefore available at such cathedrals as Durham, Beverley and Ripon. When criminals claimed refuge at such places they were often provided with a distinctive dress and allowed to wander within certain prescribed limits, the boundary beings marked by crosses. At Beverley Minster, the fugitive could wander with no fear of capture, to a distance extending a mile from the church in all directions, richly carved crosses marking the limits. Violation of the frithstoll here was considered so grave an offence it was punishable by death.

Once inside the church and seated on the frithstoll, the criminal could not be seized and there was usually a priest on watch. The period of freedom was forty days, during which time the offender could appear before a coroner to confess his crime, leave the country or accept banishment. Should the miscreant decide to foreswear the kingdom he was obliged to take the high road to the nearest seaport with no deviations, so as to leave the kingdom as quickly as possible. In the records of Beverley Minster there are hundreds of such sanctuary-seekers and it was the abuse of the privilege that finally led to its annulment. It is thought that there are only three intact chairs known to still exist in the country – one at Beverley Minster, the others at Hexham Abbey and Sprottborough in Yorkshire. However it is now thought that a stone chair, minus one arm, that can be seen in the church at Evenlode in Gloucestershire which was long regarded as a priest's chair, might well be the remains of such a frithstoll.

This custom of sanctuary influenced the dying wish of St Cuthbert, who desired to be buried at Farne Island lest if buried at Lindisfarne his grave become a place of refuge for runaways from justice, since a causeway from the mainland gave access to the island at low tide. By 1540 the Right of Sanctuary was restricted to only seven towns, later being abolished for those accused of crimes during the reign of James I and for civil cases in 1773.

Many sanctuary crosses stood very high so that the fugitive could see them from afar and be guided to safety, and very few remain. On occasion such crosses even gave sanctuary to animals, for it is known that when Basolus became a hermit in the hill country of Rheims, he was able to invoke sanctuary rights for a bear that took refuge in his cell.

Sanctuary would also be sought in churches, some having special knockers attached to their doors following those at the larger bishopric sanctuaries. Durham had one shaped as a grinning face, with large eyes and nose surrounded by curved shapes reminiscent of a 'green man', a substantial knocker hanging from either side of his jaw. The little church at Dormington has such a knocker, in this case showing the head of a grimacing feline

A sanctuary knocker at Durham Cathedral.

beast with large eyes and a ring through its mouth. This type of doorknocker is peculiar to Herefordshire and is the only example in bronze.

Should sanctuary be violated in any way, it was necessary for the church to be re-consecrated by the Bishop, with church services being suspended until such re-consecration had taken place. During the battle of Tewkesbury in 1471 two soldiers from the defeated Lancastrian army were pursued by Yorkist soldiers and approaching Woolstone in Gloucestershire they sought sanctuary in the church. However, they were put to death by their followers. It was therefore necessary for re-consecration to take place. Such crosses can be seen etched on the inside wall of the south side of the sanctuary and the north tower exterior.

Boundary crosses were often erected at the meeting of crossroads and it was here that suicides were often buried. Such crosses occasionally became known as weeping crosses. It is suggested that seeing such a cross, those passing by might be moved to sympathy for the suicide lying unburied in consecrated ground and pray for their soul.

Commemorative or Memorial Crosses

Anglo-Saxon stone monumental crosses can be traced back to early times when rough unhewn obelisks were erected to commemorate chieftains, maybe those slain in battle. It is thought the size of the stone and the difficulty in raising it would vary according to the value placed on the person commemorated. From these early stones there later developed more elaborate and ornamental crosses.

A cross of this type is to be found at Barton in Yorkshire. Erected over 1,000 years ago by the monks of Lindisfarne, it marked one of the places at which they stayed when they fled before the Danish invaders, carrying with them the body of St Cuthbert. This saint, a man from the lowlands of Scotland was a simple man who never sought power and honour for himself, and he received the call to be a missionary in a strange way. One day whilst indulging in a boisterous game with some friends a tiny child challenged him as to why he was spending his time thus. From that day he realised his was to be a life of service.

In addition to these pillar crosses are interlaced examples. These are simple stones carved into the shape of a cross and erected on a base, sometimes with engraved interlaced bands or cords. On these may be letters or inscriptions such as '"Person A" erected this cross to the memory of "Person B". Pray for his soul.' Examples of both types can be found at 180 different localities in Great Britain. There can occasionally be found crosses with incised pictures showing hunting and other scenes, along with short inscriptions, in addition to the normal religious figures. These are most often found in Scotland and Ireland. Whilst it must be assumed there were other crosses of the same date that were fashioned from wood, the vagaries of our British climate would have caused these to disappear long since.

However we do know that in 1511 one Joan Wither bequeathed a sum for the restoration of a wooden cross in the village of Reding in Kent. Also, John Nethesway of Taunton, Somerset, directed his executors by his will dated August 1503 to 'make a new cross of tree in the churchyard of St Mary Magdalene nigh the procession way'. One presumes he is referring to those processions made by the church congregation particularly at Easter and Ascensiontide. Sometimes these highly sculptured crosses erected by the Saxons are known as 'high crosses'. The earliest can be found in Scotland and date from the seventh century. Courtney Dainton, in his book *Clock Jacks & Bee Boles* tells us these crosses are sometimes known as Anglian crosses, apparently from an early belief that they were made by the Angles.

Some of these early crosses are now preserved in the body of churches in our area. In the porch of the church of the United Anglican and Methodist Church at Newent, Gloucestershire, stands the shaft of a Saxon cross. This shows worn carvings of the Sacrifice of Isaac, of David and Goliath and of the fall of man in which a serpent is entwined round the Tree of Knowledge, with Adam and Eve on either side. There are also the remains of another Saxon cross that can be seen in the church at Cropthorne, Worcestershire. This was found buried in the wall of the chancel. Its edges are adorned with a Greek key pattern, and the surface is intricately carved with intertwining foliage, lions and a creature with a long neck. It is supposed a hole in the middle may once have held a jewel.

Part of another ancient Saxon cross can be seen in the church at Tenbury Wells. It is carved with plait-work and serpents and has a cavity, thought perhaps to have held the relic of a saint.

During the digging of a grave a little to the south-east of the south porch at Mickleton, Worcestershire, a fragment of a Norman-period sculpture was found, believed to have come from a churchyard cross.

This little cross, now sited before a fourteenth-century window in the north aisle, bears a crude figure of Christ on the cross and shows his head crowned with thorns and inclined to the right. It would have been mounted on stone shafts and set upon steps, often called a Calvery. It is nude to the waist, the toes pointing outwards. Apparently the position of the feet and the number of nails portrayed (in this case, four) indicates a date prior to 1200. Standing on quite a high window sill it is not easy to see the exact carving, however there is in the churchyard a modern memorial that bears a replica of the earlier work.

An interesting feature is that the figure is repeated on the reverse side. Depending on the light at the time one sees it, there may be a better view from outside the window.

Part of a Saxon cross to be found in the church at Tenbury Wells, Herefordshire.

A very early sculpted cross, part of a churchyard cross now to be found in the church at Mickleton, Worcestershire.

It may well be that the figure was found very near the original site and in that case one figure would confront the people as they came up the steps from Mickleton, whilst the other faced parishioners coming to church from Hidcote. As the the cross was not broken it may be inferred that the order of Parliament for the utter destruction of all crucifixes and images was not always well received in out-of-the-way places. Pooley tells us that in the 1860s this fragment was to be found in the garden of the vicar, Reverend Hadow.

Of crosses set up specially to commemorate important events I'll mention just two. Although these are not in our area they do serve as good examples of this type. In 1884 Earl Granville, the Lord Warden of the Cinque Ports, erected St Augustine's cross at Northside in Ramsgate, setting it up to commemorate the landing by St Augustine that took place at Ebbefleet in AD 597. The design is based on an ancient Saxon cross and is carved with symbols of Saxon mythology and Christian saints. The north side at the top is carved with runic ornaments and monsters symbolical of the Saxon religion, while below are three panels containing the figures of St Alban, St Augustine and, in the lowest, King Ethelbert I with two angels in prayer.

Another is the Loudoun Memorial at Ashby-de-la-Zouch, erected by the people of the town in 1879 as a monument to Lady Flora Hastings, Countess of Loudon, the daughter of the first Marquis of Hastings who was much loved by the people. Sir Gilbert Scott was commissioned to design the cross, decided to do so in the shape of an Eleanor cross. Lady Flora is probably better known for a little poem she composed, referring to a visit to Ashby castle by James I, whose mother, Mary Queen of Scots, was later imprisoned in there for a short time. James arrived at Ashby with an enormous retinue that needed to be entertained in royal style, which left the earl considerably poorer when he left. Lady Flora thus recorded his visit with a poem, saying:

> The bells did ring,
> The gracious King,
> Enjoyed his visit much.
>
> And we've been poor,
> Ere since that hour,
> At Ashby-de-la-Zouch.

Hardly brilliant poetry but it says it all!

Not only crosses have been set up to remember those lost in battle. For example a large cairn of stones remembers those soldiers who fell at the Battle of Glkansnuir, or Culloden. It is said the first stone was made by a passing tinker, the cairn arising from an accumulation of stones. A cairn was the usual way to commemorate the dead in Norse countries, so there are many such remains in the country – particularly in the north.

At the end of the First World War it was decided to set up permanent memorials to the many men who perished during the fighting. Many of these memorials follow traditional designs, such as those at Chaddesley Corbett, Prestbury or Guiting Power. These have suffered from weathering during the past ninety years and it is difficult at times to differentiate between the old and the new, especially since in several cases the bases or shafts of medieval crosses are incorporated into these newer war memorials. An example of this can be seen at Chaseley, Gloucestershire, where the square step and base of the ancient churchyard cross has received a new shaft and cross head as a war memorial. Another is at Hanley Castle, Worcestershire, where the war memorial has used the shaft of an

The Loudoun Memorial, Ashby-de-la-Zouch, Leicestershire.

A modern war memorial at Guiting Power, built in the style of a medieval cross.

ancient cross. This had been found lying in a field on the Worcester Road, a few yards before Hangman's Lane, and has thus earned itself the name of 'Hangman's Cross'. When it was decided to erect a war memorial in 1922, this shaft was used. Also in the village is a cross that stands at the end of Quay Lane. The Ordnance Survey map also marks a further cross in the churchyard, but there seems to be no sign of it now.

Many of the medieval crosses that had been falling into disrepair in the past have been renovated as a memorial to past members of the community, sometimes by local people wishing to remember their loved ones in such a manner, or by important families in the area, and often by past vicars.

At Chaddesley Corbett, Worcestershire, the family of Lady Crease of Sion House renovated their ancient churchyard cross in 1904. This had been mutilated in Puritan times and the base used for many years to support a sundial pillar. This restoration was undertaken in memory of Captain H.C. Oldnall, killed in South Africa during the Boer War. Also in Gloucestershire is one to be found in the village of Down Ampney. Here the steps and shaft of an ancient stone cross have a nineteenth-century canopied top, carved on one side with the crucifixion. This was restored in memory of Paul Butler by his wife who lived at Down Ampney House, a building with fine gables and twisted stone chimneys approached by a gatehouse flanked with embattled towers, gables and turrets. There is a local legend that in the year AD 603 St Augustine met and conferred with Celtic bishops somewhere nearby, as told by the Venerable Bede. Two local fields have long been known as the Wicks, a name derived from *Hwiccas*, the ancient Saxon tribe, where it is believed the meeting took place, although it is now thought this meeting actually took place at nearby Aust

Another modern cross erected in the style of a medieval one can be found by the churchyard path of St Mary & All Saints Church at Hampton Lovett in Worcestershire. This was built in memory of Augusta Anne, Lady Pakington, whose family purchased the local manor in the 1400s. The house was rebuilt in Tudor style and in 1600 additional land

A modern cross marking the grave of Sir
Douglas Galton at Himbleton, Worcestershire.

near the site of a recently dissolved nunnery was granted to the family by Henry VIII and
a new house built there that became the principal family home.

Also modern is a cross at Himbledon, Worcestershire. Erected on five steps and with
an octagonal base, this marks the grave of Sir Douglas Galton, a soldier and engineer
who died of blood-poisoning in 1899. A child of two well-established local families, the
Galtons and the Darwins, he entered the army in 1840, aged eighteen. He was the first to
use an electric spark to explode a charge of gunpowder when he blew up the wreck of
the Royal George. On returning to this country at the end of his army career he spent
years investigating the properties of iron for use in railways and bridges, and researching
into a variety of engineering problems including drainage in London and the erection of
the Thames Embankment. His main work however related to questions of public health,
including the sanitary conditions of hospitals at home and military hospitals both here
and overseas. It was largely through his support that the Red Cross was formed.

Set on a grassy courtyard leading to the door of the church of St Nicholas at Queenhill,
Worcestershire, are the remains of an old churchyard cross restored by the addition of a
new head featuring a carving of the crucifixion. It stands on three steps and a stone
base and bears an inscription saying, 'By Thy glorious resurrection and ascension, Good
Lord Deliver Us.' A further inscription, rather worn and illegible, placed on the top steps
tells us that it was raised in pious memory of William Dowdeswell by his surviving son,
E.R.D. in 1904, in order to commemorate the restoration of the church 'as a symbol of
faith for many generations' that had become badly defaced and mutilated.

Other Crosses, including those of Absolution

One of the most unusual crosses must be that to be found in the wall surrounding
the ruins of Llanthony Secular Priory in the city of Gloucester. Once a very active

establishment, it had been built due to the fact that the original priory of Austin Canons in Llanthony Valley, South Wales, had been seized by rebels in 1136. The prior and about twenty canons retreated to Hereford where Miles d'Bohun, Abbot of Hereford, awarded them land attached to his castle at Gloucester as an alternative site. This extended eastwards to the modern Bristol Road, northwards to about halfway across the modern docks and westwards to the river. The church dominated the site which was later cut by a canal during the eighteenth century. Within the church had been buried ten generations of the d'Bohum family, hereditary Constables of England.

Unfortunately nothing remains visible today of either the church or its cloister, although there is a range of red-brick buildings thought to be the oldest surviving brick structure in the county. Set in the south end of a red-brick precinct wall, is a cross design made by black bricks, now appearing simply part of the larger pattern, but marking the spot where a wayside cross had originally stood. The fact that it was actually built into the wall indicates it was put there before the Dissolution of the priory in 1538. It does take a bit of finding!

Some crosses were said to have been erected for certain types of person. For example at King's Weston, originally in Gloucestershire but now in the Bristol area, there was a cross where sailors would pray on safely returning from a voyage. Known and used by sailors from various parts of the country, there was a niche cut into the stone to receive contributions from grateful travellers or those intending to travel who prayed for safety on their journeying.

There are also crosses erected by past kings or generals to mark victories, or as thanksgiving for safe return. One such cross can be found in the churchyard at Middleton-on-the-Hill in Herefordshire. This was erected in thanksgiving for those who served during the two world wars and returned safely.

Crosses of absolution are found in sepulchres on which an absolution is engraved. Thus in the ancient church of Butteils, near Dieppe, several exhumed skeletons were found bearing on their breasts rudely cut crosses of sheet-lead on which words of absolution occurred. In England such have been found at Bury St Edmunds, Chichester and

At Middleton there is an unusual thanksgiving cross that celebrates the safe return of all those from the village that fought in the First and Second World Wars.

elsewhere. One of a bishop, dated 1088, is still at Chichester. Sometimes the cross of absolution was not placed actually on the dead but used to induce prayers for his soul. An indulgence was offered to any who through charity should pray for him.

Such absolution promises were also granted in other circumstances. For example at Clapton, Gloucestershire, the little church of St James has on its walls the remains of a promise written on a large stone in Latin, saying that whoever shall say a prayer three times devoutly whilst on his knees will earn a reward of release after death from a thousand days in purgatory. Such promises were sometimes made to those who gave money for the building of churches and other pious works.

Consecration Crosses

Consecration crosses differ from those found in churchyards and have a completely different origin. In early times, when a church was consecrated, the bishop was obliged to anoint twelve places inside the building and a further twelve on the outside. Such crosses, usually of the Greek type, were seen by the medieval church as a defence against demons and the Devil.

Whilst the ceremony of consecration varied slightly from building to building, it did follow a general pattern. When the bishop arrived to consecrate a newly built or rebuilt church, he had to climb a ladder to every cross, which had been prepared in advance. With each cross a bracket was fitted to hold a long candle. He then anointed each cross by tracing the shape with his thumb dipped in 'chrisom' – a mixture of oil and balm. Each anointment was accompanied by his saying in Latin 'Blessed be this church' whilst clerics below sang a biblical anthem about the building of the Temple in Jerusalem. After this, burning incense was waved under each cross. Medieval pronouncements say the crosses were intended to 'scare away devils, to signify the victory of Christ and to recall the Passion' whilst the twelve candles represented the twelve apostles.

Such crosses could be carved, affixed in metal or etched in patches of plaster on existing walls or altars, or they could be painted or incised. On many occasions, but not always, such crosses were painted inside a circle, usually in brownish-red; three to a wall. On occasions, these would be at a height of some 7-8ft, high enough to be out of the reach of vandals whilst others might be on altars as at Garway, Herefordshire. Later, they were often placed on or near the chancel arch. In all events once there they should never be removed.

Many early churches had stone altars, the majority of which would have consecration crosses carved in to them. However, during the English Reformation, altars of stone were banned and replaced by communion tables of wood. These were often quite small and where used in Catholic churches and chapels could be easily converted to a tray or table if the Mass were interrupted at a time when to be a Catholic was forbidden and quite dangerous. This ban resulted in the loss of many stone altars, some being broken up, others relegated to other uses. In the church of St Leonard at Beoley, Worcestershire, there is an altar on the east wall said to have been given by the Pope to Ralph Sheldon, a Roman Catholic recusant. The legend says that Sheldon obtained permission from Queen Elizabeth to tour the continent where he visited Rome and was able to tell the Pope of the problems then being faced by Catholics in England. Since there are no consecration crosses showing on

Typical consecration crosses can be found to either side of the chancel at Overbury Church, Worcestershire.

the face of the altar today it is presumed these are beneath the slab. It is therefore thought to be one of the very few English churches to have a Papally consecrated altar.

Although the traditional ceremony took place as explained, we have also found consecration crosses in various places, at varying heights, and in various forms. These could well be of a later date when the procedure may have been diluted somewhat or placed there when a building needed to be reconsecrated. The marks vary from crude kiss type crosses to very elaborate ones and may be painted, incised or cut into the stone or walls. They can be found in church porches, on both internal and external walls or on pillars in addition to early altars. At St Andrew's Church at Sevenhampton, Gloucestershire, there is a curious passage squint near to the base of the central tower through which a view of the high altar can be seen from the north transept. The roof of this is formed from an ancient stone altar on which can be seen some deeply incised crosses, thought to be consecration crosses. Painted consecration crosses can be seen on either side of the chancel in Overbury Church, Worcestershire, and high up on the exterior of the western wall at Turkdean, Gloucestershire.

Chrisom, the word used for the mixture used by the priest to consecrate the building can also refer to a white vesture worn by the priest at a baptism. Prior to 1552, this ceremony entailed a three-fold dipping of the child by a priest wearing such a garment. The child was then wrapped in a white cloth (also known as a chrisom) to be worn until the 'churching' of the mother i.e. the ceremony of purification about a month after the birth. After this the garment would be returned to the priest. As he put the chrisom on the babe, he would say, 'Take this white vesture for a token of the innocence which by God's grace in his holy sacrament of Baptism is given unto thee'. He then anointed the child with the same mixture of oil and balm as was used to consecrate a church. The word 'chrisom' therefore came to be used for both the vesture and the pronouncement and our modern word 'christening' derives from it.

A chrisom could also be a child who died within the first month of their life as often shown on tombs and brasses, especially those of the Tudor period. The babe is shown covered by the chrisom cloth and tied around with swaddling bands, wrapped up almost like a parcel.

Gazetteer

Map references are referred to under the name of the village followed by the number of the Ordnance Survey Map, Landranger Series and the grid coordinates of the location.

Gloucestershire

Ampney Crucis. 163. 064/019
Situated on the Fairfield Road, this cross stands in the churchyard of the Church of the Holy Rood dating from about 1415. There is a further cross at end of Church Walk, opposite the church gate.

Ampney St Peter. 163. 081/015
A tall octagonal shaft, topped by a cross stands on a base and two steps. In addition to this are three sundials. One of these appears on the church tower, and there are two more ancient dials in the churchyard.

Ashleworth. 162. 812/255
The village cross, believed to be fourteenth century, is sited on the village green and stands on two square steps and a square, bevelled-edge socket-stone. The shaft bears a lantern top showing four scenes.

Aston Magna. 151. 202/357
This is a very small hamlet with no mention in any of the books we referred to. However it did have a church in the past (now a private residence) and a short way along the road we found what appeared to be the socket-stone of an old cross, set on a pile of stones at intervals facing outwards was a base appearing as a series of chevrons, set on a stone slab. From this rose part of a shaft.

Aylburton. 162. 617/019
A substantial cross of mixed styles is situated near the Cross Inn. Built of local forest stone, the main structure stands some 9ft high, is square in shape and topped by a flat stone on

Remains of a forgotten cross can be found in a garden hedge at Aston Magna, Gloucestershire.

which is a further chamfered one. Above this a further square stone is topped by another chamfered one bearing a repeat stone. In each side of the cross are large niches that could well have held full-size sculpted figures. The whole rather gives the appearance of a sort of square shrine. This cross was repaired around 1841 and was moved back a few yards from its original position in the 1960s as it had become a traffic hazard. It is thought this cross originally supported another stone from which rose a tall shaft topped by a Latin cross as at Clearwell. The church at Aylburton was moved to the foot of the hill in 1857 together with its fifteenth-century stone pulpit.

Badgeworth. 163. 901/192

Shaded by firs and yews in the churchyard stands a cross set on two steps, the lower of which has a deep drip. These support an original socket-stone with chamfered angled corners. Pooley wrote that the cross was much defaced, so we can be grateful to Ellis Viner, the then vicar, who restored it in memory of his parents, Joseph E. Viner and his wife Ann, in 1897.

Barnsley. 163. 077/051

It is known that there were several crosses here in the past and it is thought one was worked into steps leading to a granary. In Pooley's time there were portions of a shaft, probably of the same cross, preserved in the garden of the clerk. Originally it had three large steps and a base of about 3ft square. Nothing is visible today.

Bisley. 163. 903/060

Mr Rimmer describes this cross as being unlike any other, saying, 'It has the appearance of being erected over a well… but there is no trace of a spring now'. Pooley also calls this a cross, saying that it 'may easily be mistaken for a handsome sepulchral monument'. He describes this as being 'an upright hollow hexagon, formed by six three-centred arches, supported on rounded columns, with beaded capitals and square plinths. On this tier rises a hexagonal pyramid, built on a corresponding number of smaller arches with

Although thought to be part of a cross in the past, it is now supposed this is a well-head in the churchyard at Bisley, Gloucestershire.

very deep mouldings… with a small cross of modern date on the top.' He does, however, query the fact of it being a cross, and speculates as to whether this erection could be a twelfth-century well-head as later research rather confirms. There is a local tradition that one dark night the priest was asked to take communion to a dying parishioner whom he never reached. His body was eventually found down the well that was later built over in order to prevent it happening again. In the process, it's said, Bisley was excommunicated – with burials being forbidden to take place there for two years. During this time Bibury Churchyard, some eighteen miles away, was used instead. Alms for the poor were left in the nooks, the monument being known locally as 'The Bonehouse'.

Blacksworth (No longer in existence)
Mr Pooley tells us that on a hill, within a few yards of the turnpike gate leading to Crews, was a small dwelling-house that had in former days been a Catholic chapel dedicated to St Anthony. In the highway some 200yds west of the church there once stood a circular column of stone raised on an octagonal base known as Don John's Cross. It's said this was placed near an adjacent house when the church was built. There is a local tradition that the corpse of Don John (perhaps Domini Johannis), a noble Spaniard, rested at this spot on its journey to interment, probably in Spain, from the port of Bristol.

Brockworth. 163. 891/170
All that remains of the old cross in the churchyard here is a portion of the base, now hollowed out and planted with flowers.

Bromsberrow. 150. 742/336
Set on two steps are the remains of a thirteenth-century cross. Mr Pooley tells us that during restorations in 1857, a sculptured stone said to be the head of an old cross was found built into the east wall. Thought to be Norman and of early date (probably the late thirteenth century) this measured 12in diameter and was 3½in thick, being grooved on

its circumference. It was carved with a crosslet between four fleurs-de-lis, alike on both sides. Since the church is dedicated to the Virgin Mary it is supposed the fleurs-de-lis was intended as a symbol of her. The steps support a square socket-stone from which rises a square to octagonal shaft bearing a wheel-head cross. In the churchyard today are the remains of an old cross, bearing a head as described, a plaque stating that it was renovated in 1832 in memory of Joseph Cambourne Smith.

Buckland. 150. 082/360

In the churchyard, standing on two square fourteenth-century steps and a square socket-stone with drip moulding, is a modern shaft topped by a Celtic cross. It is thought there was originally another step.

Calmsden. 163. 045/085

Standing on an eminence above a spring which gushes into tanks by the roadside is an impressive early fourteenth-century wayside cross standing on four steps and a socket-stone. This supports a tall, slightly tapering hexagonal shaft terminating in a cube whose sides face the four compass points. This is thought to have originated from the time of the Knights Templar who were at nearby Quennington. The knights were gifted property at Calmsden by Mabel, the wife of William de Laga and also by Richard, the son of Robert de Calmsden. It is thought the cross could have been erected in accordance with ancient usage in order to mark who owned the lands.

Charlton Kings. 163. 965/204

In the crowded churchyard of St Mary's Church are the remains of a late fifteenth-century cross, restored in 1913. Two steps of stone blocks support a chamfered base on which stands a tapering octagonal shaft some 7ft tall. This is topped by a modern head with what I was

An early fourteenth-century wayside cross at Calmsden, Gloucestershire, set up over a spring.

told were sculptures of the crucifixion, the Madonna, a saint with a palm, and a king with a sceptre, but these were difficult to make out. In Pooley's time the shaft was topped by a square head on top of which was a round ball, both being of modern construction. By the main entrance to the lych-gate of the churchyard stands the head of an ancient sundial on a newer pillar. This bears a round stone ball – could this be that from the earlier cross?

Chaceley. 150. 855/306

In the churchyard of St John the Baptist is the square base of an old cross holding an octagonal, tapered modern shaft surmounted by a cross that is now used as the village war memorial. The village stocks can be found in the church itself, together with an old drum that was part of the orchestra in the days before the building had an organ.

Cheltenham. 163. 952/227

To the north-east of the St Mary's Church stands an 8ft-high cross set in an irregular octagonal socket-stone mounted on three steps. Following the destruction of the capital, the block was utilised by fixing a sundial thereto. This was later removed and a four-gabled capping substituted. It is thought this cross is from the time of Edward I but is more likely to be fourteenth century.

Chipping Sodbury. 172. 728/823

Facing the long wide main street is a war memorial cross dating from 1919 that has part of an early cross incorporated into it. There is known to have been a market cross from around 1370 which was replaced in 1522.

Cirencester. 163. 023/021

To the side of the magnificent church dedicated to St John the Baptist stand two fine crosses – old and new. The new one has a small crucifixion and the Madonna and the old one, an ancient market cross, is set on a stone base with beautiful arcading and fading angels. There were a series of standing crosses around the town in medieval times, mainly located at road junctions, but of six described by Pooley in 1868 only one survives – the high cross relocated to the West Market Place in 1927.

Clapton-on-the-Hill. 163. 162/180

Situated in the churchyard of the Church of St James is the base of a churchyard cross. Surrounded by grass and covered in moss it is difficult to spot (and to be honest there is little to see) but the little church itself is worth a visit.

Clearwell. 162. 571/080

Here at the crossroads in the centre of the village stands a splendid cross. Gothic in style, it is built of grey Forest of Dean stone and thought to date from the fourteenth century. Standing on five large steps is a square base with a niche to each side, probably once containing sculpted figures. A further square base supports a slender shaft crowned with a floriated cross. A drawing by Pooley shows that in the mid-1800s only a small part of the shaft still existed, but this was restored during his time at the instigation of Caroline, Countess of Dunraven, a benefactor of the village.

Coberley. 163. 966/158

Near the south porch of St Giles Church is the base of a fourteenth-century cross. Standing on a square socket-stone is another, its top being bevelled and with chamfered angles. This is worked into a circular plinth from which rises about 2ft of the octagonal shaft, the whole now rather worn. This church is known for its association with Dick Whittington. His mother, Lady Joan Berkeley, married Sir William Whittington after her first husband died an outlaw a few years after their son, Richard, was born. It is said Dick Whittington spent much of his childhood at Coberley Hall, the Berkeley family home. The site of this house is in a field to the south of the church.

Colesbourne. 163. 004/134

This is another church built on the edge of the grounds of a large estate, in this case the family home of the Elwes family. The church has been standing for some 900 years and has a rare medieval stone pulpit, one of only about sixty that have survived from the fifteenth century. This is built in the style of the wooden wineglass type with a tall fluted arcaded stem. The wall of the chancel holds a large collection of lead memorial plaques to many of the Elwes family and it was interesting to note that amongst the names of the Friends of Colesbourne Church, who had worked an attractive altar frontal displaying a snowdrop scene, was a certain Carolyn Elwes. Near the south porch stand the remains of a churchyard cross. Set on three weighty steps composed of a series of stones is a chamfered base and about 12in of an octagonal shaft.

Colne St Dennis. 163. 085/109

By the churchyard gate are the steps and base of an old cross with a new shaft, while behind the building are two short memorial stones bearing Maltese crosses typical of Templar tombs.

Condicote. 163. 151/283

There is a cross set in the centre of the village alongside a walled green area wherein can be found the village pump.

Daglingworth. 163. 993/050

This churchyard cross is set on two heavy steps, the lower having a broad drip stone. On these is a square socket-stone with a moulded fillet running around the base, from which rises a much weathered octagonal shaft. It is thought to be extremely old, probably Anglo-Saxon.

Deerhurst 150. 871/299

It is known there was once a cross here, which has unfortunately long since disappeared. However the village is well worth a visit for it is one of only two places in the country to possess a pre-Saxon chapel and a Saxon church. The chapel has at sometime had a beamed Elizabethan farmhouse built onto the back of the tiny building and was only rediscovered in the nineteenth century by Reverend George Butterworth. It is thought to have been built on the orders of Odda, a friend of Edward the Confessor. The Saxon church, not far away, is also well worth a visit.

The cross at Didmarton, Gloucestershire, has a socket stone with figures at each corner.

Didmarton. *172.811/876*

In the churchyard of St Lawrence stand the base and part of the shaft of a fourteenth-century cross traditionally known as 'the Preaching Stone'. Set on a square step topped by a smaller one arranged diagonally, stands an octagonal base. In each corner are half-figures, sculpted in high relief and thought to represent the four Evangelists. The church itself, of typical Georgian style, is light and bright and has a rare three-decker oak pulpit painted apple green.

Dowdeswell. *163. 001/199*

Pooley tells us that the cross that formerly stood in the churchyard here was removed around the turn of the nineteenth century.

Down Ampney. *163. 098/965*

In the village are the shaft and steps of an ancient stone cross with a nineteenth-century canopied top, carved on one side with a crucifixion scene.

Driffield. *163. 074/998*

Whilst the church was being restored in the mid-1800s, a square block of stone was found built into the porch. It is believed this could have formed the socket of a cross, especially since a fragment of a shaft was discovered at the same time.

Duntisbourne Rouse. *163. 985/061*

An early English medieval cross with its slender shaft stands some 8ft tall and is mounted on two square steps and base in the churchyard of St Michael's Church. This probably dates from the 1400s but was moved from elsewhere to its present position west of the south porch. Beneath the church a dark stairway leads to a small crypt with a barrel roof and a deep splayed Norman window, thought to have served as a chapel for the celebration of Masses for the dead. Such crypts are exceedingly rare in small village churches, although several of the larger Cotswold churches have them. Following the Reformation they were usually used as charnel houses and sealed off.

Dursley. 162. 759/977
Here in the centre of the town is a stone-built market house resting on twelve arches.

Eastleach Martin. 163. 202/054
Almost hidden beneath a holly tree in the churchyard are the remains of a cross standing on two rather decayed steps and a narrow socket-stone holding part of a shaft. This appears to be at variance with the description given in Pooley's book, when he describes it as being on a single basement step. This church is now in the care of the Churches Conservation Trust

Eastleach Turville. 163. 202/052
To the south side of the church are the remains of what is thought to be a fifteenth-century churchyard cross standing on two steps. A small socket-stone supports a tapering square shaft. Pooley tells us that on his visit in the mid-1800s the shaft had been dislodged and left lying on the grass.

Ebrington. 151.183/400
It is known there was formerly a village cross here, which in the 1860s was being used as a cheese-press in a neighbouring farm-house.

Edgeworth. 163. 948/060
In the churchyard of St Mary's Church, accompanied by a selection of trim box hedges, stands a restored fifteenth-century churchyard cross. A 4ft 10in square step supports another some 3ft square and 15in high with a deep overhanging splayed drip. From this rises a modern obelisk some 5ft high carrying a carved head. It would appear this has been more recently restored since in the 1860s the shaft was topped only by a tenon.

Elkstone. 163. 966/123
It is known there was an imposing high cross here in the past.

Gloucester (No longer in existence)
A print by Vertue shows there was a splendid cross in this town, the drawing showing it to be of great height. A top storey had niches that held sculpted figures of kings and queens. It is said to have been erected in the reign of Richard III but was probably older. It is thought this was destroyed when an Act of 1749 allowed for the removal of some buildings and the enlarging of certain city streets, the cross being pulled down in 1750.

Gloucester – Llanthony Secundula. 162. 820/180.
The surrounding wall has the sign of a cross marked in black bricks as part of a pattern. This marked the spot of an old preaching cross.

Guiting Power. 163. 095/245

An attractive war memorial built in the ancient style is accompanied by a row of golden Cotswold cottages. It stands on a series of steps in the centre of the village. Pooley tells us there could have been a cross at a place called 'Stumps Cross' in the neighbourhood, but I have been unable to ascertain any further information.

Hampnett. 163. 100/157

This little village stands on a hill overlooking the Fosse Way. In the churchyard is a chamfered square base bearing a rather lopsided part of an octagonal shaft of a cross. In the 1860s there was also a worn base of a simple cross remaining on the village green. The church itself, dedicated to St George, is well worth a visit. It has much Norman masonry and a splendid chancel arch. However its true glory lies in the walls that are a riot of colour, a nineteenth-century re-creation of medieval art showing just how a church would have looked then. This work was undertaken by the Reverend William Wiggin, the incumbent at the time. Apparently in the *Cotswold Church Monthly* of 1892 he claims to have painted it himself, but it is thought it more likely it was done by Clayton & Bell, a Bristol firm of stained-glass makers. It is however known that the work was undertaken in 1868. It seems the villagers at the time weren't enamoured with their vicar's artistry and set up a fund to pay for its removal. Fortunately not enough money was raised and most of the murals remain, for which the present-day residents of Hampnett, together with most visitors to the church, are extremely grateful.

Harescombe. 162. 837/104

This small but lovely little church, consecrated in 1315, has an unusual bell tower, a Norman font with a plain round bowl on thirteen clustered pillars and a Jacobean oak pulpit. In the churchyard stand the remains of the steps, base and part of the shaft of what is described as a preaching cross.

Haresfield. 162. 810/104

There was once a village cross here but it was broken up at the start of the nineteenth century by the vicar, Archdeacon Rudge, who used the pieces to mend the road!

Hatherop. 163. 153/051

Set on the edge of a garden on the main road through the village and protected by metal railings, the remains of an old cross stands on four steps. A bevelled socket-stone supports about 18in of shaft.

Hempsted. 162. 813/170

The cross here stands in the village itself. It is in good repair but today looks rather incongruous, surrounded by modern housing. Pooley tells us that when Mr Lysons came to reside at Hempsted Court in 1836 there were only the steps remaining. The shaft was then discovered under soil in the churchyard and he had it restored to its original position. The upper portion of the shaft and the cross surmounting it were carved under his direction and placed on the top. It is now set on three steps, of varying thickness, has a chamfered base, and a shaft bearing a Celtic cross. The church itself is thought to have been built in the fifteenth century by Henry Dene, a prior of Llanthony Abbey, who could also have set up the cross here.

Hillesley. 162. 770/897

Pooley tells us that part of the shaft of a cross was discovered in pulling down the old cottage that replaced St Giles Cross.

Horsley. 162. 838/980

In a small area divided from the churchyard of St Martins Church, is an ancient cross now bearing a poppy wreath and converted to a war memorial. Since there was a small priory in the village centuries ago, long since vanished, it is likely this fourteenth-century cross was originally set up by the priors.

Huntley. 162. 717/198

Set on the pavement to the side of the road where the A40 (T) meets the A4136 road stands a double socket-stone and part-shaft of a cross, about which I have found little information.

Iron Acton. 172. 680/835.

A unusual shaped cross stands before the church of St James the Less. This was set up in 1390 by Robert Poyntz in memory of his grandmother, and is thought to be one of the few remaining crosses set up for the sole purpose of acting as a preaching cross.

Kempsford. 163. 161/965

The church of St Mary the Virgin is something of a surprise with its lofty space, painted and gilded beams and brightly coloured windows, which when the sun shines, speckle

The remains of a wayside cross at Huntley, Gloucestershire.

the interior walls with brilliant colours. Even more colourful is the roof of the tower, and the painted organ pipes. Across the road from the church, in line with the church's lych-gate, is a new graveyard wherein can be found the base and part-shaft of an old cross. Pooley tells us this was to be found standing in the centre of the village in 1692. His drawing, made in the middle 1880s seems to be identical to one he found in a cottage garden. This must therefore have been removed to the churchyard relatively recently and although he describes the shaft, about 3ft high and standing on a hexagonal socket-stone, as being octagonal, weathering makes it now appear round.

Latton. 163. 092/955

On the road from Cirencester to Cricklade (part of the old Ermine Street) is a side turn-ing leading into the village. Standing on the pavement here are the remains of an ancient cross. A small plaque attached to this tells us it is the remains of a preaching cross that was restored in 1982. It stands on two steps and has an octagonal inwards-sloping base in three parts. On each of the four sides is a niche-shaped pointed top. This supports a tapered shaft that seems to have lost its head. Since none of the books to which I have referred mention either the village or the cross, I can only presume this has been rediscovered recently.

Letchlade (No longer in existence)

It is known there was once an old cross standing in the market place here.

Little Rissington. 163. 190/200

Near the porch door of St Peter's Church is the ivy-covered stump of an old yew tree, beside which is the rather insignificant square base of a churchyard cross. In the churchyard a large area is set aside for the burial of men who died whilst stationed at RAF Little Rissington from 1938-1976.

A recently re-erected cross at Latton, Gloucestershire.

Lydney. 162. 630/029

The fourteenth-century cross standing at a T-junction in the centre of the town strongly resembles that at Aylburton, although standing on a higher flight of steps. Mr Pooley considers both could have been designed by a foreign artist, probably an Italian, as it is known that such artisans were employed in the building of crosses elsewhere in the country. An illustration in his book shows the cross terminating at the top of the niched base, but certainly by 1907 the cross had been restored to its present state. The town was granted to Sir William Wintour following the Armada. His house was destroyed during the Civil War, and it is likely the cross was dismantled at the same time.

Maisemore. 162. 814/216

Near the south porch of the St Giles Church stand the base and steps of a fourteenth-century cross, now scheduled as an ancient monument and cared for by English Heritage. I'm told this was taken from St Michael's Church, Gloucester, in 1956. It is known that a cross once stood on a bridge built about 1200 that bore the following inscription in Latin and Norman French: 'In honour of our Lord Jesus Christ who was crucified for us, William the son of Ankertill of Lilton began this cross'.

Newent. 162. 724/259

In the south porch of the United Anglican & Methodist Church are the remains of a Saxon cross found in the churchyard. This shaft has worn carvings of biblical stories. I was told that in the church is a tablet sculpted in sandstone that has on one side the crucifixion with the figure of a bishop or abbot standing amid a group of ape-like grotesques. Although this shows a likeness to Saxon carvings, it is thought to be Norman as it bears in one corner the name of Edred, one of the twelfth-century founders of Little Malvern Priory. Unfortunately, in spite of calling on several occasions the church has always been closed (increasingly a sign of our times I'm afraid).

Newland. 162. 552/095

In the churchyard of All Saints Church (known locally as the Cathedral of the Forest) stands a restored cross, the work being undertaken in memory of Margaret Birt in 1864. All that remained of the old fourteenth-century cross were its five steps and a massive base into which the shaft was formerly fixed. Following the shaft's disappearance a shorter stone replaced it, showing signs of the customary sundial marks. In the base is a sculptured niche that was probably used as a reliquary, or a receptacle for the Pyx. At the time of the reconstruction it was found that the steps had sunk, so the stones were carefully marked and reset in their old positions. The restorers were careful not to disturb any weathering appearing on their surface. Unfortunately the base was too badly spoiled to be retained so was copied. The new top consists of three stages, the lowest a tapering irregular octagonal shaft and the next has canopied niches facing in each direction that contain angels with outstretched wings, the whole topped by a foliated cross.

North Cerney. 163. 018/078

In the churchyard is a restored handsome shaft on three steps crowned by a twelfth-century wheel-head cross.

Notgrove. 163. 110/200

To the left of the Tudor doorway to the church of St Batholomew is the octagonal base of a thirteenth-century cross. The base has alternate angles chamfered to a square, from which rises a short portion of the shaft. This church is an absolute gem, containing a Norman tub font and fragments of carved Norman stones. There are also medieval figures of the Whittington family, who lived at the manor house. One of the great treasures is a large embroidery executed in wool, worked in gross and petite point. Conceived as a means of raising funds to repair the church tower in 1936, the family of Sir Alan Anderson of the nearby manor worked on it until 1954. Designed by Sir Alan's eldest son Colin, two generations of the family of both sexes took part in the work that took some eleven years to complete, for it was laid aside during the Second World War. The canvas is in twenty pieces and is based on the original Norman reredos and scraps of remaining colours now behind the altar, which the embroidery covers. The landscape between the arches shows the church, village and manor and the remainder is composed of symbols representing family members.

Prestbury. 163. 970/240

The cross in the churchyard here appears to be modern in the main and stands opposite the entrance to the church. Standing on three octagonal steps and a solid square base with bevelled corners is a square-topped octagonal shaft capped by a Raguly cross.

Rendcombe. 163. 018/098

This church, dedicated to St Peter, is set in the grounds of a present-day college. It was once the home of the Lord of the Manor, Sir Edmund Thame, a rich sheep farmer and clothier. The building was almost completely rebuilt at the beginning of the sixteenth century. A rare treasure is a Norman font depicting eleven of the twelve Apostles, each identified by the tools of his trade. A twelfth space, that for Judas Iscariot, is left blank. In the churchyard stand three weighty stones, similar to that seen at Colesbourne, thought to be standing on an original holy site dating from about AD 800. They thus predate the earliest church here. These three steps supporting a square socket-stone are thought to be original and in the mid-1800s held about 1ft of shaft. Today this socket-stone holds a rather stumpy Celtic cross, thought to have been put there about 100 years ago. It is thought the original shaft, probably destroyed in the Puritan revolution, would have been a lofty one.

Rodmarton. 163. 943/981

Mee states that during repairs in 1926 a stone with interlaced carving was found in the wall, thought to be the remains of a Saxon Cross used in building the Norman church. However, we could find no sign of this. The interesting little church of St Peter does have on its fine old door a hand-wrought iron knocker. Could this perhaps be a sanctuary knocker?

St Briavels. 162. 559/046

It is known that near the south porch was a cross situated in the churchyard of St Mary the Virgin. This was removed in 1830 when the new tower was built.

Saintbury. 150. 117/402

At the foot of Saintbury Hill there is an old village preaching cross standing alongside Middle Hill Farm. This is thought to have been a resting place for funeral processions before starting up the steep hill to the church. Standing on four square steps is an octagonal socket-stone with a canted upper edge, thought to date from the fifteenth century. From this is a tall square to octagonal shaft restored in the early 1800s when a modern sundial cap top surmounted by a Latin cross was added. Prior to this a painted stone pineapple ornamented the top.

Sapperton. 163. 947/035

Here are the remains of a fifteenth-century churchyard cross. Set on a base of dressed stones, a 6ft square of masonry, now cracked, supports a square base with circular dressings above, chamfered angles and an octagonal tapering shaft some 5ft high. A tenon on the top shows there was once a head.

Sevenhampton. 163. 032/218

There is a consecration cross incised into an ancient altar stone now forming the roof of a wide squint in the thirteenth-century church of St Andrew.

Snowshill Manor. 150. 097/337

In the garden of Snowshill Manor, at one time the home of Charles Paget Wade and containing his extraordinary collections, stands what appears to be an old cross. This, however, was created by Mr Wade who restored the house and garden in the 1920s. It is said to have been made from a farmyard gatepost.

Snowshill village. 150. 097/337

At the top of the churchyard in the village there is a cross. Standing on three square steps at the highest point of the churchyard is a square to octagonal socket-stone. From this rises a slightly tapering shaft topped with a lantern head. Although this gives the appearance of an ancient cross, I'm told it was erected as a war memorial at the behest of the rector, Mr Reynolds, who commissioned Frederick Landseer Griggs to design it. The design was discussed with Mr Wade at Snowshill Manor. The stone from Stanton quarry was donated by Sir Philip Stott and cut and erected by George Diston Senior with his brother Albert, and Jack Coppinger. The inscription reads, 'In Memory of those from this village who died for their country in 1914-18'. More recently it featured in the film *Bridget Jones Diary* which was partly filmed in the village!

South Cerney. 163. 049/972

There is a village cross standing on a junction leading to the village. It stands on three steps (parts of which are original) and has a square to octagonal socket-stone. From this rises an octagonal shaft with a modern ball top, to which had been added a slender Latin cross of iron.

Stanton. 150. 069/342

In the centre of this charming Cotswold village stands an ancient cross, its eighteenth-century octagonal shaft rising from three square twelfth-century steps, the bottom one of which has a pronounced dripping stone. A broached socket-stone holds an octagonal shaft capped by a square block, which in the mid-1880s supported a round ball topped by a Tau cross. This head, whilst still preserving its square block, is capped by a sundial, its cross now a Latin one. Only the lower features are old.

Staunton. 162. 551/126

The remains of what is believed to be a fifteenth-century village cross are located on a grassy bank sheltered by lofty trees opposite the church where the main road splits. It stands on four eight-sided steps of sizes varying from 2–4ft high. The sturdy socket-stone is some 3ft square, its top chamfered into an octagon. On a further octagonal plinth stands the fragment of a shaft, the whole built from the same forest stone as other crosses in the Forest of Dean.

Stow-on-the-Wold. 163. 191/258

A market cross that dates from the 1400s stands in the square. Standing on the edge of busy roads its substantial base supports a tall shaft terminating in a tabernacle top on which appear sculpted panels dedicated to events and people of importance to the town.

Teddington. 150. 964/340

Sited about 100yds west of a roundabout between Evesham and Cheltenham is an unusual signpost. In the past signposts often had arms terminating in finger-pointing hands, often referred to as 'finger posts'. This example has six hands with fingers pointing directions where five roads meet. Although it retains its original form, it was moved a short way some years ago in order to facilitate traffic movement. It is believed to have been erected on the site of an old wayside cross at the beginning of the 1600s by Charles Attwood, a husbandman in Teddington Wayside Cross. A small metal plaque states the following:

At Teddington Hands, Gloucestershire, is an old finger post, a reminder of how signposts would have appeared in the past.

Edmund Attwood of the Vine Tree
At the first time erected me.
And freely he did this bestow
Strange travellers the way to show

Since generations past and gone
Repaired by Charles Attwood of Teddington

Succeeding members of the Attwood family have updated this rhyme when repairing the cross later in 1868 and 1876.

Temple Guiting. 163.091/278
In Pooley's time there was said to be a cross at a place called 'Stump's Cross' in the neighbourhood.

Tibberton. 162. 757/219
Mee tells us that for some years there was a preaching cross, known as the Butter Market that originally came from Gloucester. This was brought to Tibberton in the eighteenth century but was returned during the 1930s. In Pooley's time there a fragment of the octagonal shaft of a cross in the churchyard, on the south side of the church.

Tortworth. 162. 704/933
This fourteenth-century cross is opposite the old north door of the church and is mounted on three square steps and a square socket-stone. The tapering octagonal shaft, some 7ft high, is mounted on an upper bed. In the 1860s the cross was surmounted by a modern four-sided capital and ball, but is now topped by a fancy cross. Nearby stands the Tortworth Chestnut, a Spanish chestnut tree thought to be some 800 years old.

Tredington. 163. 904/295
The church here is set alongside an ancient main road known as the Ridgeway. On 3 May 1471, Edward IV marched along this, spending the night before the Battle of Tewkesbury at the old manor house formerly sited here. In the churchyard, to the south of the church, is an elegant fourteenth-century cross standing on four square steps. These support a slender and elegant tapering shaft, some 12ft tall, cut from a single piece of stone. It is thought there was once an escutcheon or small crucifix attached. Pooley tells us it was thought that a person of eminence was buried beneath the cross.

Tresham. 162. 792/918
This attractive little village church stands on a small hill, beyond wide lawns interspersed by a few gravestones. To the right of the building, just inside the gate, is what appears to be an ancient stone pillar set on a single square step and an octagonal socket-stone. A square block, ornamented with a dial, once capped the shaft but this has latterly been replaced by a triangular piece of stone.

Turkdean. 163. 108/174

Built by Robert D'Oligi during the Norman period as penitence for a life of cruelty and greed, All Saints Church is thought to be one of the oldest in the Cotswolds. High on the external west wall is what appears to be a consecration cross, although since there are also signs of other apparently reused ancient stones. I was not able to ascertain whether this cross is original to this church or not. Was there was a predecessor on the same site?

Twyning. 150. 893/360

The remains of the old cross lie piled up in the churchyard to the left of the gateway leading to the church of St Mary Magdalene. In the jumble of stones can be seen a square step, a smaller but deeper base, two parts of the shaft and various other smaller pieces.

Westbury-on-Severn. 162. 717/139

A lady chapel once stood between the tower and the church here. From this came the base stone of the shaft of the twelfth-century cross, now set up in a triangle formed between the churchyard and an inn. The base of this is obviously that described by Charles Pooley. It is in such a condition as to appear to have been recently renovated, but the head bears the date 1887, obviously commemorating Queen Victoria's Jubilee. I have been unable to ascertain whether the present cross is an amalgam of other original crosses, for in Pooley's time there were still the sockets of three old crosses in the parish. It was thought there were originally many others, used to mark the thirteen tithings.

Westcote. 163. 220/206

In the churchyard here are the very weathered remains of what is believed to be a late thirteenth-century cross. Now only a sculpted base remains. It is believed this had a six-sided base with capitals and arched recesses. In each are sculpted figures now so well worn that they are almost impossible to make out, although one might be a soldier standing with a shield propped by his right foot and holding a spear in his left hand. Another is believed to be a prelate in mitre and cope, and another a monk. Pesvner says he considered the cross to be late thirteenth century and that it may have been a wayside or village cross from Coombe Baskerville, a place formerly within the parish but long since demolished. There is a legend that it could have originated from Bruen Abbey where a son of the powerful Baskerville family, who held Westcote, was a monk in the twelfth century. These remains of the cross were moved to their present position early in the 1800s, having been discovered as part of a garden wall.

Weston-sub-Edge. 150. 129/406

On the right-hand side of the inner door in the porch is a dial stone. Etched into this is the symbol for the Holy Trinity and a small consecration cross. We were told there was also a cross sited where four roads met.

Whittington. 163. 014/207

In the churchyard of this delightful little church dedicated to St Bartholomew, stands an ancient cross. The base appears to be early fourteenth century, with the shaft thought to be fifteenth century. Contrary to most designs, the base doesn't appear to be on steps, although on the day we visited the churchyard was snow covered. It is, however, of unusual design being octagonal but with large rounded buttress-like broaches on the alternate faces. The shaft, almost 10ft high, is also octagonal, tapering to the top to a stone circle with a tenon that once probably held a head. The socket and shaft are probably of differing dates, the former early fourteenth century and the latter late fifteenth century.

Winstone. 163. 966/094

Hidden away at the end of a track through fields stands the church with its squat saddleback tower. In its churchyard is the broken octagonal stem of a fourteenth-century churchyard cross standing on a broad plinth, two steps and a further central chamfered socket-stone. This cross is similar to that at Sapperton. This ancient church has a fourteenth-century porch, its flagstones worn by time and countless worshippers, and a medieval font. When we called early in February, sunlight beamed through a small window into the tiny chancel, lighting the altar adorned by an attractive altar frontal.

Woolaston. 162. 586/993

The church of St Andrews stands in a rather isolated spot at the end of a lane with the River Severn nearby. It has a squat-gabled solid little tower with a pyramid cap, this being almost all that remains of the old building restored extensively during Victorian times. In the churchyard, set on a large square socket-stone, stands part of a shaft of an old cross. This rests somewhat precariously on a bump in the grass. Could there be steps beneath it?

Woolstone. 150. 961/302

The church of St Martin de Tours has two consecration crosses. One, a cross set inside two circles, is etched into an external wall at the west end of the building on the north west buttress of the tower. The other is a Maltese cross inside a circle, painted in the usual red/brown manner, and appears in the chancel on the left side of the south window.

Herefordshire

Abbey Dore. 161. 386/304

Although it is known there was once a cross here, we were unable to find any trace and I gather that even in the early 1920s it was almost impossible to find.

Almeley. 149. 333/515

This church has an early thirteenth-century tower with a clerestoried nave, aisles and porch of the fourteenth century. The chancel screen and loft is modern but the old rood loft stairway can be seen. In the churchyard stands the square step of the old churchyard cross, on which is a square socket-stone with bevelled corners. On this a collection of rounded pebbles has been placed. The short octagonal shaft has a turned, tumbler-shaped wooden addition, now badly worn. It seems there could have been a sundial inside this since a short, wounded metal spike has a horizontal cut along the top.

The cross at Almeley, Herefordshire, has an unusual appendage at its head. Inside there seems to be the remains of a sundial head.

Allensmore. 149. 466/358

Beside the church porch stand three stone steps, the lowest some 8ft square. On this a square socket-stone with a slight bevel supports a 3ft-high octagonal shaft with a square stone cap for a missing sundial. In 1605 this tranquil spot was the centre of some controversy when the then vicar, Richard Heyns, refused burial for Alice Wellington who, as a Catholic, had died excommunicated from the Church of England. Some fifty people gathered and forcibly laid her to rest in the churchyard, resulting in arrests and violent outbursts that lasted for some six weeks.

Aston Ingham. 162. 683/235

To the south of the nave stand the remains of a churchyard cross. A worn socket-stone with pyramid corners and a diagonal lozenge top stands on top of a square step. This supports a square of which the lower part is original, a 1911 restoration giving a heavy foliated cap and cross.

Aymestrey. 149. 425/651

The church here is dedicated to two saints – that of St John the Baptist and St Alkmund (a little known Anglo-Saxon saint of the eighth century). In the churchyard stand the remains of a late (probably sixteenth-century) churchyard cross on tiered octagonal-shaped steps. There appear to be five steps, although this is difficult to assess since at the time we called these were surrounded by a protecting ribbon and a notice explaining that, 'This ancient preaching cross is in the process of being fully restored thanks to generous donations from local people, English Heritage and other grant funding bodies'. Mr Watkins tells us that in the 1920s this cross stood on three octagonal steps with a square to octagonal socket-stone holding an 8ft shaft with an octagonal capstone surmounted by a melon-shaped ball and iron cross-spikes to the four quarters.

The cross in the churchyard at Bishops Frome, Herefordshire, is so completely covered by ivy it is impossible to describe it.

Ballingham. 149. 575/316

We found this church situated by a farmyard at the far end of a road that took us through a scattered village, way out in the countryside. This fourteenth-century cross is set on three mossy steps, the top one being of solid stone that served as the base for the shaft. This shaft (not the original) had been reformed with a stone cap serving as a sundial in the eighteenth century. The churchyard appeared to be set on a slight promontory, the wall around it almost circular. The church itself was locked when we visited.

Bishops Frome. 149. 664/484

Set amongst hop-fields and orchards close to the River Frome stands the large church. In its churchyard, set to the south east of the chancel some little way from the porch, are the remains of a churchyard cross. Watkins tells us this stands on three circular steps and a flat circular socket-stone with a modern octagonal shaft with a flat top for a missing sundial. He remarks that in 1929 all were in bad condition. Today ivy so completely covers the steps, socket-stone and even the shaft itself that it is impossible to check on the condition.

Blakemere. 149. 362/411

To the south of the chancel in the churchyard stands a cross on four steps. On this rests a square to octagonal socket-stone with curious tucked-in corners and a niche some 9in high on the northern face, as is usual. From this rises a tall square to octagonal shaft with pyramid corners and a modern tabernacle head that has shallow panels on three sides with a deeper one on the fourth side. This contains a figure of the Virgin and Child and is surmounted by a small Latin cross.

Bodenham. 149. 530/509

In the churchyard of St Michael & All Angels stands the original base of the churchyard cross on three square steps. A church leaflet leading us along a churchyard trail tells us that the shaft has been replaced by a gable stone and a cross from the church roof.

A village or market cross stands on the green at a road junction leading to the church. Here is what is believed to be a cider mill-stone supporting a square to octagonal socket-stone with short pyramid corners. From this rises a 12in octagonal part-shaft thought to have been brought from Dewdales Hope quarry around 1860. It is believed the base is probably a survival of a market cross that preceded a wooden market shed that stood on the spot some years ago. This cross is accompanied by a modern, tall war memorial cross. The memorial is topped by a Latin cross standings on three steps, with a two tiered octagonal socket-stone.

Bolstone. 149. 551/327

Watkins tells us that in 1929 there were the remains of a cross to the south of the porch. This had no steps, a square to octagonal socket-stone with gradually bevelled corners, and a roughly octagonal shaft about 3ft high with the top shaped to a cross, which probably had a sundial. He also tells us there was a date of 1701 and the initials 'TW' and 'CW' on the sides of the shaft. We were unable to confirm this since the church is in the grounds of a farm and on both occasions we called it was securely locked with the yard full of roaming animals.

Bosbury. 149. 695/435

Beside the path leading to the lych-gate is a fourteenth-century cross with a modern shaft and head, standing on a square base and three steps. Until 1796 it stood opposite the south porch. Although said to be a preaching cross, there seems to be no evidence to support this. In 1903 the remains of Edna Lyall (Ada Ellen Bayly) were buried at its foot. The Victorian writer of best-selling romantic novels used the village as the setting for her book *In Spite Of All*. Her brother was the vicar here. Watkins states that when the churchyard cross was moved to its present site in 1796 the movers were so surprised to find a great boulder of unhewn stone embedded in the structure that they placed this stone beneath the tower and recorded the fact.

Brampton Abbotts. 150. 601/263

Unfortunately, the church of St Michael & All Angels has been closed due to the roof being in a dangerous state, and we were told the cost of repairs was so great that nobody really knows what will become of the building in the future. It would certainly be a crime should it be allowed to deteriorate, for it has Norman origins when the village belonged to the Abbots of Gloucester. In the churchyard we found a lovely old cross amongst many tombs and gravestones in a variety of styles. Standing on three tiered square steps, a square to octagonal socket shaft bears a niche with a plain ogee top. This supports a new shaft and modern head.

Bredenbury. 149. 610/564

It is known there was once a cross that stood before Bredenbury Court.

Bredwardine. 149. 334/445

The fact that this site is almost circular suggests there was a pagan site here before the Christian church. An early Welsh document known as the *Book of Llandaff* refers to a church known in Welsh as 'Llan Iuanabui', the description of the site leading to the conclusion this was Bredwardine. Watkins describes the cross here as having no original steps and an octagonal socket-stone some 3ft high, elaborately moulded with ogee top and a notch the full depth of stone. He wonders if this may have been a niche as there was a stone step against it. There was no shaft. At present there is just a pile of stones with the socket deeply cracked.

Bridstow. 160. 584/248

Sited on a narrow road leading towards Hoarwithy, the church of St Bridget's has within its churchyard a series of octagonal steps. These are now extremely worn and there appear to be only three. However, Alfred Watkins mentions the octagon-bevelled base with a round hollow on four top corners, as standing on four steps. The short shaft then held a modern sundial of which the gnomon is now missing.

Brilley. 148. 261/492

In the churchyard are the remains of an old cross standing on two square steps, the top one of which is solid stone. The socket-stone is square with rounded corners. This supports a shaft some 3ft high, which has an eighteenth-century cap and a sundial. The names of Mr C. Wilson and J. Davies, churchwardens of the time, are engraved on the face of the dial.

Burghill. 149. 479/445

In the churchyard, near to an area set aside for the burial of ashes, stands a tall churchyard cross on four steps and a modern shaft terminated by a Latin cross. Inside, one of the church treasures is a lead font, one of only thirty-eight remaining in the country.

Clehonger. 149.464/379

This church has been closed on the several occasions when we've called but to the east of the chancel is a churchyard cross, thought probably to have been moved from elsewhere. It stands on two steps, its socket-stone supporting a tall shaft topped by a Latin cross. In Watkin's time the socket-stone had an 8in hole that contained a piece of broken shaft. With the church being closed we were unable to have sight of an altar table in which we were told there were three consecration crosses.

Clodock. 161. 326/275

This cross is almost hidden amongst a great mass of individual gravestones – there are over 1,000 in the churchyard. It stands on two tiers of smaller stones on which there is a square socket-stone with bevelled corners at the top. There is no shaft, but a modern sundial vase shape column rests on the top. This was restored by W. Lewis, churchwarden in 1819. Although this shaft is of obvious sundial design there appears to be no sign of any gnomon ever having been here. The church itself is a beautiful old building with a 700-year-old font, a handsome wooden western gallery built for the use of an orchestra

Restored in 1819, the cross in Clodock churchyard, Herefordshire, gives every appearance of having been turned into a sundial.

and choir and panelled box pews set within two aisles. There is also an ancient three-decker pulpit adorned with scrolls and flowers and covered by a canopy.

Coddington. 149. 718/426

In the churchyard of All Saints, south of the chancel, stand the remains of a thirteenth-century churchyard cross, constructed of local stone. It stands on five moulded steps with a chamfered socket-stone and coping, in which there is a niche with a trefoil top. The part square to octagonal shaft is topped by a Latin cross placed there in Victorian times.

Colwell. 150. 739/422

The church of St James with its thirteenth-century aisle and nave, fourteenth-century tower and an even older plain font, is some way from today's village since most of this was not built until the advent of the railway in 1861. South of the chancel in the church-yard are the remains of a churchyard cross standing on three square steps. The square to octagonal socket-stone with hollow bevel corners supports the stump of a shaft bearing a round-headed niche with pinnacle decoration.

Cradley. 150. 736/471

Just outside the porch and standing on two steps is a square socket-stone with slightly bevelled corners. In this is a roughly octagonal shaft that we're told was turned upside down when it was restored in 1887 and a sundial was added. A plaque attached to this states that the sundial was 'restored in commemoration of the Jubilee of Victoria, Queen of the Realm, June 21.1887'. Incised along a top square stone holding the dial are the words 'Tryth, Troth, Tyme'.

The cross at Colwell, Herefordshire.

Craswell. 161. 281/362

This little church is somewhat isolated, standing as it does in the shadow of the Black Mountains with extensive views down the valley. The building is an absolute gem, remaining very much as it was in times past. Standing alone in the grassy churchyard are the remains of three steps that appear to be slowly sinking. There is no socket-stone as such but a square hole in the top step is consistent with there once having been a wooden shaft. Like other Herefordshire churches, there seems evidence that the area was once used as a Fives court. More surprising there is a tradition that cockfighting may even have been carried on there.

Dewsall. 149. 485/334

This little church stands in the grounds of Dewsall Court. The church was closed and appeared to be in need of some care and attention. The gate leading into the porch was in a sorry state, although there was a brand new entrance gate to the churchyard itself. To the south of the nave were the remains of a cross, two square steps supporting a square socket-stone, its corners slightly bevelled with round-headed niche. Into a large socket hole, part of a shaft had been haphazardly inserted from where it leaned rather precariously.

Docklow. 149. 564/575

This little church was closed when we called but just to the south of the porch was a square to octagonal socket-stone with pyramid corners and water channel moulding at the top edge. It is thought this was to hold a wooden cross.

Dorstone. 161. 315/417

The old preaching cross to the south-west of the church of St Faith's was rebuilt on its original site in 1906 in memory of a much loved pastor. An entirely new cross with octagonal steps and head – a copy of that at Upton Bishop – was erected. Watkins tells us that before this date there were only some square steps of a decayed cross with no socket-stone or shaft, that were to be found to the north-west of the church. The cross now stands on three square steps and a 2ft 3in square socket-stone with slightly bevelled corners and a round-headed niche. This supports a square to octagonal shaft. The church itself was rebuilt in the 1800s but retains remnants from the old building.

A local legend has it that many years ago on All Soul's Eve, a man by the name of Jack of France was on his way home when, on hearing noises in the church he peeped through the keyhole. There he saw the Devil reading out the names of the people who were to die during the coming year, one of which was his own. Deeply shocked he died shortly afterwards! Near to the village can be found a cromlech known as Arthur's Stone.

On the green near the school can be seen what is thought to have been a village cross, now a sundial. The square to octagonal shaft, almost 12ft high, is topped by a sundial consisting of a diagonal brass plate with pegs top and bottom as indicators.

Dulas. 161. 371/293

In the past a chapel stood in the grounds of Dulas Court. This was demolished about 1860. However, there still remains a square-built pedestal with a tier of steps. There is a square to octagonal socket-stone supporting a shaft that appears to have had a sundial mounted onto it, although we didn't get to see it.

Eardisley. 148. 312/491

This charming and interesting village, one of those described on the 'Black & White Trail' in north-west Herefordshire has in its church an intricately carved font, worked by local stone masons. The work represents the struggle for the soul of an individual between the power of Evil and the saving grace of Christ. In the churchyard are the remains of a cross. There are no steps, but an octagonal base narrowing to a modern shaft with a wheel-head top, bears a plaque telling us that this was restored in 1906.

Eaton Bishop. 161. 443/391

In the churchyard of St Michael & All Angels, to the side of the porch and south of the chancel, stands a cross bearing an attractive four-hole modern finial head. This restoration took place in 1880. Two steps support a plain octagonal socket-stone from which rises the shaft, with its head.

Ewyas Harold. 149. 387/287

In St Michael's Churchyard, south of the porch, is a late medieval cross, restored in 1868. This stands on three octagonal steps. There is a square to octagonal socket-stone with a coping from which rises a square to octagonal shaft with pyramid stops. In the 1920s this was topped by a cross. A metal plaque bears an inscription saying 'in memory of...', the remainder being too difficult to read. The shaft and lower part of the base are original, as is the site on which it stands.

The cross at Ewyas Harold was restored in 1868, although the attached plaque is too weatherworn to be able to decipher in whose memory this work was carried out.

Fownhope. 149. 581/342

On the north side of the church are two square steps of solid stone on which rests a square to octagonal socket-stone in two pieces, the lower one having a bevelled top to take a square stone changed by a humped stop to an octagonal top. When Watkins visited it had a shaft topped with a Latin cross but by 1917 this was without its shaft. Today, however, it appears as complete.

Foy. 149. 598/283

I understand there used to be a cross north of the nave, but that the remaining octagonal socket-stone was moved to a nearby wall. I could find no trace of this when I visited and the church itself was closed.

Ganarew. 162. 529/163

In the churchyard to the south-east of the chancel stands a churchyard cross with a modern shaft and head on a three-tier set of square steps. There is no socket-stone and it seems this was originally designed to hold a wooden shaft.

Garway. 161. 454/224

I understood there to be two crosses in the churchyard here but could only find one that was tucked away at the back of the church. Only the socket-stone appears to be old, the shaft and head being a late nineteenth-century restoration. The church, sited amidst fields and sheltered by its hill, has to its side the foundations of a round church of the Knights Templars, one of the earliest of their buildings in this country. The present building has Norman masonry and a medieval altar with four consecration crosses fitted into a modern altar table. There is also a consecration or sanctuary cross incised into a wall. It is thought that near the high road, well west of the church at the entrance to a farm, was another old religious site where there may well have been another cross.

Goodrich. 162. 572/190

Just outside the porch can be seen the remains of a medieval cross. Four square steps, the bottom some 9ft square, support a square to octagonal shaft with bevelled corners. In Watkins' time this carried a square cap dated 1692 and held a sundial. It is possible that the original shaft was a wooden one. The cross now holds a plaque saying that it was restored in 1911 in commemoration of the coronation of King George V.

Hampton Bishop. 149. 559/380

Behind St Andrew's Church, to the north of the nave, is a preaching cross standing on three octagonal steps. The square to octagonal socket-stone has ribbed hump corners and a projecting niche with a pent-roof. The square to octagonal shaft supports a thin circular capstone on top of which is a modern fleur-de-lis cross. When we visited a couple of years ago this had lost its highest portion and also part of the trefoil decoration on the cross shaft. However, the church guide tells us there are plans to reinstate this when funds allow. A photograph taken in the 1920s shows the top of the cross intact but that on the left is missing. It would appear this type of cross is particularly susceptible to breakage. This cross is thought to be one of those erected for outdoor worship during the Black Death.

Hentland. 162. 543/263

This church dedicated to St Dubricius is very isolated and was one of the early churches that continued for centuries in the original British manner. In the churchyard to the left of the path, standing on a square step and a 3ft-high socket-stone with a high bevelled top edge, is the remains of an old cross. This dates from the fourteenth century but it was severely damaged in the religious arguments of the seventeenth century. This was later restored but the square to octagonal shaft with a bevelled top has its original head in tabernacle form with one main ridge roof with side pentroofs. The figures are now very worn and difficult to recognise, but that on the west side bears a crucifixion with Saints Mary and John and on the east side, the Virgin and Child. To the south there is a cleric, probably St Teilo, and on the north a bishop with a mitre thought to be St Dubricius himself.

Hereford (Black Friars' Cross). 149. 510/397

A true preaching cross set up around 1246 by the Black Friars and sited in the grounds of the remains of their monastery dating from 1276. This is to be found in Widemarsh Street in gardens attached to Coningsby Hospital.

Hereford (White Cross). 149. 492/406

A market or wayside cross standing in the centre of a very busy roundabout on White Cross Road just over a mile from the High Town on the A438 towards Brecon. It stands on seven hexagonal steps forming the radius of a circle. From these is a column with panels containing alternate shields. This fourteenth-century cross was set up in 1365 as a thanksgiving for the passing of the plague by Bishop Charlton, whose arms appear on it and who is buried in Hereford Cathedral.

The White Friars Cross, Hereford.

Holme Lacy. 149. 569/347

This church, dedicated to St Cuthbert, stands some one and a quarter miles from the village and is reached by a long narrow lane. Very isolated, it stands near Holme Lacy House – now owned by Herefordshire County Council and cared for by the Churches Conservation Trust. This imposing building bears witness to the Scudamore family who, during the seventeenth and eighteenth centuries, paid for repairs and new furnishings. They remained as patrons of the living from medieval times until 1909, the building having many memorials to the family. Near the south porch is a stone churchyard cross, probably dating from the fourteenth century. It stands on four tiers of square steps on which is a square socket-stone, its sides sloping slightly outwards and with a deep bevel at the top. There are two symmetrical deep notches or hollows on the west side that seem to have been made for the knees of worshippers. The steps appear to be more recent, as does the upper part of the square to octagonal shaft, which appears to be mounted on part of the original. The remainder of the cross, together with a Latin cross, was added as a war memorial restoration.

Holmer. 149. 505/424

The church, now almost part of the city of Hereford, stands alongside a busy road. In the churchyard standing on four steps is a fourteenth-century square to octagonal socket-stone adorned at the corners with ballflowers, and there is a niche – unusually facing east. From this rises a modern square to octagonal shaft and head in one piece, the whole standing about 15ft high. The church was closed when we visited.

Kenderchurch. 149. 403/284

This church stands high on a hill on the A465 and as far as we could see the only way was to walk through fields to the left of the sawmill. South of the church porch stand the remains of a medieval cross, a square step bearing a square to octagonal socket-stone with hump corners. In this is an unusually placed niche with a pointed top. The shaft is rectilinear, its head being of monumental style. Only the socket-stone is original, the remainder being restored during the nineteenth century. Again, the church was closed.

Kentchurch. 161. 419/256

South of the nave of the church there stands a modern cross on an ancient 5½ft square step. On this, in front of the socket-stone, is a rather rare kneeling block. This rectilinear socket-stone has no bevel or shaped corners and bears a shaft and head in one piece, with Celtic bosses added in 1887.

Kings Caple. 149. 559/288

In the churchyard of St John the Baptist's Church stands an old cross on three octagonal steps bearing a chamfered square socket-stone with hump corners. This supports a modern shaft and is topped by an even newer mitre-shaped head bearing a sculpted Latin cross, an earlier one having been broken following the fall of a tree. This cross has long been known as a Plague Cross.

Kingsland. 149. 447/612

In the churchyard, south of the porch is a circular stone step on which rests an octagonal socket-stone, its top slightly bevelled. This supports a square to octagonal shaft that obviously once held a sundial.

Kington. 148. 291/567

Here, the remains of the old churchyard cross have been made into a focal point in a garden of remembrance for the interment of ashes. It stands on two octagonal steps on which rests a square socket-stone with a niche. From this rises part of a shaft. The church guide tells us that on special occasions – when congregations proved too large to be accommodated in the church – they would gather around the medieval preaching cross.

Knill. 148. 291/604

In this church is an attractive thirteenth-century font, its panels carved with stars, crosses and quatrefoils and on the walls is an impressive collection of hatchments. In the churchyard is a fourteenth-century cross standing on three square mossy steps. These support a square socket-stone with wheat-crease corners with a niche with a cusped top. From this rises a modern narrowing square to octagonal shaft with a squared head topped by a cross.

Ledbury. 149. 713/377

There are two spots in the town known as the Upper Cross and the Lower Cross that suggests crosses may have been there, especially as the second is close to the seventeenth-century Market House. There is a sixteenth-century market building on a long established market site.

Leominster. 149. 495/591

In grounds adjacent to the large and impressive priory church stands a 'black & white' market house on wooden struts. Built on a long-established market site, this sixteenth-century building was moved to its present position in 1853 when it was rebuilt as a private residence. Watkins tells us that Blacklock, in a book on Leominster, records a cross or shrine at St Botolph's Green, a mile out on the Hereford road. There are place names called the Iron Cross, the Golden Cross and the Red Cross, the last at the bridge over the Pinsey in Broad Street, all suggesting there were crosses there in the past. About a mile away is a place known as Barons Cross and whilst it is known it was used as a meeting place for the barons, it is not known if there was ever an actual cross there.

Linton. 162. 660/253

Standing on a square step, a short socket-stone is supported on each corner by a pointed smaller stone. From this rises a square to octagonal tapering shaft with a pyramid cross head. Between the cross and a surrounding short square, stone wallflowers have been planted. This is now the war memorial. Just beside the church porch are two immense yew trees near which, in Mee's time stood the basis of the cross.

Little Dewchurch. 149. 529/317

This mainly modern church with a fourteenth-century tower has been closed for some years. But in the overgrown churchyard, just south of the porch, stand the remains of a churchyard cross. A square socket-stone having a niche stands on worn square steps. The base stone holds part of a square to octagonal shaft, once a sundial.

Llangarron. 162. 530/212

Whilst there are no remains of an actual cross, the large churchyard attached to St Deinst's church has an unusual sundial erected in 1911. This is comprised of the top of an old spire set on a circular stone base thought by some to have been constructed from the foundations of an old preaching cross.

The fourteenth-century cross in the churchyard at Knill, Herefordshire.

Llanrothal. 161. 471/186

We found this church isolated in most beautiful countryside and reached through fields. A tiny porch leads into a beautifully preserved little chancel with a medieval stone altar on which stand three crosses given to the church around 1995 and nearby, an unusual lectern. By the tall Gothic chancel arch is a Jacobean or early Charles I pulpit and among dark box pews is a charming little font. The church, now in the care of the Churches Conservation Trust, issues a guidebook telling of its history and shows a photograph of the building in its dilapidated state before major renovations were carried out in 1921. Within the churchyard is the step and large socket-stone of a churchyard cross. Watkins tells us that when he visited in the early 1900s there were three square stone steps, a square to octagonal socket-stone with bevel corners and a broken shaft. But when we visited there was no sign of these, although there were some large stones almost hidden beneath brambles and in the porch were two pieces of what is thought to have been the crosshead. The guide explains that until the Black Death in 1348–89 the church was surrounded by houses, with a road running nearby and a mill standing by the river.

Llanveynoe. 161. 303/313

In the south wall of the church have been inserted two ancient memorial stones, probably dating from the ninth or tenth centuries, indicating there was a very early cemetery there. One of these depicts an early type of crucifixion, the other showing early symbols for Christ. A further stone cross was found by Watkins lying below the church, he helped the local vicar to re-erect this in the churchyard. There is no known history, but it is thought to date in or before the fifth century. Whilst the original position of the cross is unknown, a range of stone seats outside the church wall on the south side suggest this could have been a true preaching cross, the seats allowing for a congregation. The cross itself is a plain monolith with two short arms similar to those found on Dartmoor, is of local sandstone and has a groove running from top to bottom. The latter is thought to have been carved relatively recently.

A sundial erected in 1911 has been set on the top of an old spire at Llangarren, Herefordshire.

Llanwarne. 149. 505/281

Set in a delightful village, through which runs the Gamber brook, are the charming ruins of a beautiful old thirteenth-century church. Unfortunately due to regular flooding the church was abandoned in 1864 and a new Victorian building erected close by on higher ground. The floor of the old church of St John the Baptist, formerly St Dubricius, was progressively raised over the centuries to more than 3ft above its original level, whilst burial in its churchyard was only possible if coffins were weighted, for the ground was waterlogged even when the swift flowing little brook kept within its banks. A fifteenth-century stone-tiled lych-gate still remains, as does the stone tower rebuilt in the fourteenth century. South of the chancel stands part of the shaft of a churchyard cross set into its original square socket-stone. Earlier this would have stood on two square steps with hump corners. The remains now stand on a bed of slabs.

Lugwardine. 149. 551/410

To the south of the nave in the churchyard and standing on three steps (part of which are new) is a square to octagonal socket-stone with wheat crease corners. The shaft and head was added when it was restored in 1909 by the vicar. Unfortunately the plaque is now impossible to read. The church itself was closed when we called.

Madley. 149. 420/387

A preaching cross stood, until recent times, at the crossing where the road leading to the side of the church meets the main road. This was moved in 1996 to the opposite side of the road since its original position was of great hindrance to traffic. The two-tier octagonal shaft topped by a Greek cross is set into a square base standing on three tiered steps. The earlier cross would have been topped with a sculpted head showing a crucifix. Since Madley had a market in early times, it was probably held around this cross.

In the churchyard to the south of the west end of the building are the remains of a cross. This is set on a square step supporting a square to octagonal socket-stone with hollow corners and topped by a small hollow bevel. In this is a niche with a plain round head. There is a square to octagonal shaft topped by moulding but not cap. The head of the cross is thought to be original and was replaced in 1916 and shows on one side Christ with his arms extended, whilst on the other is the now almost obliterated figure thought to be the Virgin Mary.

Mansell Lacy. 149. 425/455

South of the porch of St Michael's Church stand the remains of a medieval cross standing on four tiered octagonal steps, and a two-staged octagonal socket-stone with a niche. The lower part of the shaft is original, while the upper, smaller diameter half with its capital and Latin cross have been restored. The church itself has recently been tastefully renovated to provide both a church and a community centre.

Mathon. 150. 733/458

This ancient little church, in the folds of the Malvern Hills, has a history dating back to the days of Ethelred the Unready (968-1016). The present building dates to around 1100 when it is thought services were probably taken by a monk from Pershore Abbey.

We were told that just in front of the porch stands a socket-stone in which there is a canopy decorated niche that appears to be slowly sinking. The church guide tells us that:

> At the base of the west door there is a flat stone larger than a tomb stone and without an inscription that is surmised to be a 'Hiring Stone'. Before people could read or write and knew nothing of agreements or contacts, farmers requiring workers would place coins upon the stone and whoever picked them up would be hired. Taking place near the church made the practice sacred and thus binding on both master and workman.

Michaelchurch Escley. 161. 316/341

Entering the church through a sixteenth-century porch, one is faced by a fascinating painting showing a large figure of Christ surrounded by craftsmen's tools dating from the late fifteenth or early sixteenth century. To the south of the tower is all that remains of the old churchyard cross – three square steps with no socket-stone, although a hole in the top step shows there was once a wooden shaft.

Middleton-on-the-Hill. 138. 541/646

To the right-hand side of a path to the south gate is a sundial. At the east end is an unusual war memorial in that it gives thanks for the safe return of the men of the parish who fought in the two world wars.

Mordiford. 149. 571/375

To the side of the entrance porch a medieval cross has had a new Latin crosshead mounted on its 11ft slender octagonal shaft. It stands on three octagonal steps and a socket-stone with a niche that has projecting sides and canopy. The square to octagonal shaft is now topped by a modern cap and a Latin cross. This restoration was carried out some time after 1918.

Much Birch. 149. 504/304

The church here has undergone a complete modernisation and now has an open, airy, well-lit interior. At the entrance are glass doors incised with pictures of St Mary and St Thomas a Becket, to whom the church is dedicated. An earlier church had been demolished in 1835 and replaced by a larger building in Georgian style. In the churchyard is a tall cross, obviously a reconstruction although apparently on an original base. It was moved to this site when a new shaft was added as a memorial to Reverend W.L. Groves, vicar from 1916-33. In 2004 a gravedigger unearthed a decorated head of the original cross that was apparently still on the spot where it fell. This featured a bishop, the crucifixion, and an apparelled apron, all in niches with the fourth side indecipherable. This has been dated to the third quarter of the fourteenth century, and as it is thought that one of the figures is Thomas a Becket. It is believed the cross was probably erected at the time when the dedication changed to the joint appellation. It is planned to reinstate this old cross when it's possible to keep it safe.

Much Cowerne. 149. 618/472

Ancient lanes that were once drovers' routes lead to an isolated church by farmyard buildings, now converted into attractive dwellings. This is very much Elgar country for

Sir Edward, arguably England's most famous composer, cycled the lanes in and around the village and claimed the area a great source of inspiration. Standing to the south of the chancel on two square steps (the lower one now almost hidden by the surrounding grass) is a square to octagonal socket-stone, its corners low down and rather chipped. From this rises a square to octagonal shaft with a pyramid stop for a missing sundial.

Much Dewchurch. 149. 482/311

In the churchyard of this Norman church, with its thirteenth-century saddleback roof and Jacobean pulpit, is a large cross bearing a plaque stating it was restored by John Tourney Parsons, the vicar for twenty-eight years. There follows the quote, 'In love unwearied, in labours abundant, he rested July 23rd. 1878'.

Much Marcle. 149. 657/327

In the churchyard of St Bartholomew's Church, south of the chancel, stand the remains of a fifteenth-century churchyard cross on four octagonal steps. There is a heavy socket-stone topped by thick moulding from which rises a broken shaft. Nearby is a vast and ancient yew, its lower branches supported on a kind of pergola. A seat inside the 30ft trunk will hold seven people.

Orcop. 161. 474/262

This little church of St Mary, lost in lanes and wooded hills has in its churchyard a medieval cross with two steps, in need of restoration when we saw it. On them rested a square stone socket-stone with a niche having a projecting hood all round, which it is thought might have been a holy water stoup. From this rises a square to octagonal shaft. This cross

The cross at Much Marcle, Herefordshire, is thought to have been used as the centre of a market in the past.

was apparently removed from beside the porch at the time of the restoration of the building and placed further away when new paths were cut. It's thought the shaft was used sometime as the base of a sundial.

Orleton. 149. 495/672

Standing in the churchyard on four tier steps, this cross has a square to octagonal socketstone with hump corners and a niche with a pointed top. This base holds a square to octagon, rather weather worn, shaft, some 7ft tall, topped by a square cap bearing an iron pin.

Pembridge. 149. 391/581

The market hall in this ancient village, with its oak-beamed houses and inns, has been restored and is scheduled as a national monument. It is of simple construction, a stone tiled roof standing on eight wooden pillars but which shows the progression from stone marker to Tudor market. The church, one of seven in the county with detached towers, has a striking campanile.

Pencoyd. 162. 516/265

This isolated church has in its churchyard what Mee refers to as 'something of the old churchyard cross', but this is difficult to describe since it is thickly covered by ivy. The church itself is locked.

Peterstow. 162. 564/248

On a mossy square step in the churchyard here stands part of a square to octagonal shaft of a churchyard cross, surrounded by spring flowers when we visited.

Pipe & Lyde. 149. 502/441

This church is sited on the busy Hereford road on a corner plot. In the churchyard the old grey church has as company the remains of a fourteenth-century cross standing on two tiered steps. The square to octagonal socket-stone has a pyramid stop on two corners and flat bevel stops on the remaining two. It also contains a moulded-topped niche. The cross is moulded at the top and has a thin octagonal base on which a short octagonal shaft with a flat round cap is attached in order to house a missing sundial.

Preston-on-Wye. 149. 383/424

The church of St Lawrence is to be found at the end of a narrow country lane that leads to the river. In the churchyard, near an attractive wooden porch with a decorated Norman doorway, are the remains of an ancient cross. Part of the shaft rises from a large square socket-stone base containing a plain round-headed niche. It is thought the shaft originally held a sundial. Although the church was largely rebuilt in the nineteenth century, it retains much of its thirteenth-century material.

Putley. 149. 646/376

The small church is hidden amongst orchards in a leafy hollow and has in its churchyard the remains of an old cross. This stands on three steps, a square to octagonal socket-stone with a plain, pointed niche. The square to octagonal shaft has a pyramid stop and bears

Putley Cross, Herefordshire, has its original head showing figures on either side.

the original head with the sculpted figure of Christ on one side and the Virgin and Child on the other. There are also two figures to either side, thought to represent St Andrew and a Bishop, these being rather more worn. On the day we arrived, 31 January, an annual service to commemorate the restoration of Charles II to the throne was taking place.

Ross. 162. 598/241

The sturdy market hall here stands at the top of the town. Built in the traditional octagonal design for such buildings, it has an open area with six arches on each side and two at each end. Due to the slope of the site on which it is built, the building is supported by steps at one end. Above this are a series of rooms now housing an interesting heritage centre and a display area for local arts and crafts.

In the nearby churchyard of St Mary the Virgin stands a cross that marks the communal grave of those who died from the plague during the outbreak of 1637.

Rowlestone. 161. 374/271

South of the nave of the church of St Peter stand four tiered steps of substantial size, the top being of solid stone. These bear a square to octagonal socket-stone with hump corners. This cross was restored in 1905 in memory of a George William Atlay, a priest murdered in Africa. Although his father was Bishop of Hereford it seems nobody knows of his connection with this church. He was apparently killed whilst serving as a missionary in Malawi, when he refused to shoot at an invading tribesman even though he was carrying a loaded gun when he died. The rectilinear shaft has a cable moulding running up it, and a head bearing cross keys and cockerels.

St Margarets. 149. 353/338

At the foot of the churchyard here stands an old cross on square steps. These form the base from which the shaft rises, there being no socket-stone. The square to octagonal shaft has a cap for a missing octagonal sundial. Since this shaft lies in a socket smaller than is usual it is thought this was originally a wooden cross – fragments were found in the socket-hole during the 1920s. This church is an absolute gem containing an original oak rood screen.

St Weonards. 162. 495/243

In the churchyard of the church dedicated to the saint of the same name stands a sturdy cross set atop a large socket-stone some 3ft high, octagonal in shape with moulding at the top. In this is a niche with a pointed head. On to this is a small square to octagonal socket-stone with hump corners and a bevelled top surmounted by an octagonal shaft complete with what appears to be modern cap and a sundial with its gnomon.

Sellack. 162. 565/276

This church is the only one in England to be dedicated to the seventh-century St Tysilio. He was born in Shrewsbury, his father being King of Powys. When he became a monk, to the displeasure of his parents, he fled to Brittany. He established a monastery at a place now called St Suliac, dying there about the year AD 650. This church is well worth a visit, with some beautiful views of the River Wye, but again is rather remote. It has Norman beginnings and an imposing three-tier canopied pulpit. It is one of three Herefordshire parishes where for several centuries past, pax cakes have been distributed following the Palm Sunday service. In its churchyard stands a renovated, tall medieval cross, topped by a Latin cross with diminishing ends. Standing on three worn steps is a square to octagonal socket-stone with humped corners and holding a niche with a rounded head and from this a square to octagonal shaft with pyramid stops. All but the lower part of the cross is thought to be original.

Sollars Hope. 149. 612/331

The churchyard cross here dates from the fifteenth century and was repaired with a modern shaft when it was made into the war memorial. It stands on three solid steps (of which only two are now visible) and has a square socket-stone with bevel corners and containing a niche with a pointed top. From this rises a tall shaft – restored to its full height with an ornate modern cap and Latin cross. This cross is thought to have been erected in order that congregations could meet in the open air at the time of the Black Death. The church of St Michael's itself is strongly connected with Dick Whittington whose elder brother, Robert, is thought to have financed the building.

Stoke Lacy. 149. 621/494

Set low into the ground, just beside the porch, is a square to octagonal socket-stone with pyramid stops and a niche with a pointed top. A really poor example of a cross, but it's good that this small remnant has been retained.

Sutton St Nicholas. 149. 533/453

Here the old tombstones have, in the main, been tidied and to the side of the church is the base of a fifteenth-century cross. This socket-stone has chamfered corners and a large square hole that once held the shaft.

Nearby, in fields alongside the main road leading into Hereford, stands Wergin's Stone. This is not a cross but a megalithic standing stone. It has been surmised this could have been used by early Christians as a gathering point. It is now protected by metal railings, its true origins unknown.

Tarrington. 149. 618/407

Set in a churchyard are the remains of a fourteenth-century cross to the south of the nave. Standing on two square steps is a large socket-stone with a bevelled top in which there is a pyramid-topped niche surmouted by a thin octagonal plate. This holds a square to octagonal shaft with a modern cap and a sundial.

Tedstone Delamare. 149. 695/585

A narrow footpath runs alongside the grounds of Delamere Court to the church – set high on a hill and surrounded by magnificent views. It is thought humps and bumps in a field between the court and church indicate an earlier medieval hamlet. This was probably swept away when the house was built, an event that occurred in many places during the eighteenth and nineteenth centuries.

In the churchyard is a square socket-stone reduced part way up to a smaller square standing on a square step. Littlebury's *Directory* tells us this was repaired in 1629 and was altered to support a sundial in 1718. It was later restored in 1856 and the original head is surmounted by a Celtic cross of modern design.

Tretire. 162. 520/239

To the south of the nave are three square steps that support a square to octagonal socket-stone with wheat-crease corners and a slight bevel to the top. This bears a niche with a decorated pointed head and with a hood over it. The square to octagonal shaft has pyramid corners and is topped by slightly larger capstone and a floriated circular head. In the later 1920s the shaft was much shorter and its capstone supported a round stone ball.

Tyberton. 149. 380/399

To the south of the nave, and standing on three square steps, is a plain square socket-stone. Into this is set a square to octagonal shaft and the head, beneath a sloping gable roof with a roll apex and ridge. This follows the same design as that at Madley, with Christ on one side and the Virgin and Child on the other, both being well preserved. The head was found on a chancel gable and was replaced in 1916.

Upton Bishop. 162. 650/272

Watkins reports that in 1860 fragments of a wheel-head cross were found and placed on a shelf in the Norman doorway inside the church, and that this was recorded by Reverend F.T. Havergal in his *Memorials of Upton Bishop* and that no other part of any churchyard cross remained. However there is in the churchyard a cross to his memory, serving as a reminder of the ancient cross. This, together with the crosses at Much Dewchurch and Dorstone, are very similar – except that the former has a niche. In the churchyard there is also a modern cross to the memory of Miss Frances Ridley Havergal, the hymn writer.

Vowchurch. 149. 362/365

An unhewn block of local stone stands near the porch. It is thought this could be the base of a medieval preaching cross. However, there is no true evidence for this and the base is too slim to have supported the weight of a large cross, neither is it shown in a known drawing of 1820. In a photograph of 1902 it appears to bear a small sundial. There are no steps and the base stone is a rough, unworked boulder. The shaft, roughly octagonal, was surmounted by a squared cushion cap with a sundial in 1917 but this disappeared shortly afterwards. Watkins states that the stone was originally a mark-stone, since the stone is close to a ford over the River Dore on a track leading to Turnaston. However, there is no evidence to say if and when the shaft was placed on the stone to convert it into a cross. The shaft today is held together by two metal rings.

Walterstone (Does not appear on OS Maps)

To the south of the nave and standing on a square step is a square socket-stone with ornamented hump corners. Into this is a square to octagonal plain shaft with a chamfered stop.

Wellington. 149. 496/482

The large church, dedicated to St Margaret of Antioch, stands on a raised area before which, to the south of the nave, is a cross set on four octagonal steps. On these rests a square to octagonal socket-stone with elephant hump corners and a tall square to octagonal shaft with pyramid corners.

Welsh Newton. 162. 500/180

South of the chancel in the churchyard of St Mary the Virgin stand the modern shaft and head of a cross set on three square medieval steps and a square socket-stone with a bevelled top supporting a tall shaft with pyramid corners. This was either wholly or partly made new when a capital and cusped Latin cross was added. Nearby is an elaborate gravestone commemorating John Kemble, a Catholic priest born at nearby St Weonards in 1599. Acting at a time when Catholicism were forbidden, he was arrested in 1786 on the orders of the Bishop of Hereford, taken to Hereford gaol and charged with saying Mass at Pembridge Castle. He was found guilty and, although over eighty years old, was hanged on Widemarsh Common. He was beatified in 1929 and canonised in 1970. Nearby is a grave thought to be that of a Knight Templar or Knight Hospitaller, discovered in 1979.

Weobley. 149. 401/519

Here in the churchyard of St Peter & St Paul is a cross with a modern shaft and head. Standing on five medieval steps is a square to octagonal socket-stone with pyramid corners at the foot and moulding at the top. This contains shallow panels on three sides with a niche with a projecting, ogee top. The short square to octagonal shaft is headed by a Latin cross, added in the nineteenth century. On the church porch is a modern replica sundial, a copy of one dated 1663 which bore the initials of the churchwardens.

Westhide. 149. 586/441

To the west of the church of St Bartholomew, close to the road, is a cross that is a curious mixture of ages since its shaft dates from the fourteenth or fifteenth century whilst its

At Westhide, Herefordshire, the cross is a mixture of ages.

scalloped roughly octagonal capital is topped by a twelfth-century cap that was probably taken from inside the church. Standing on three circular stone steps is a circular socket-stone containing a niche with an open top, now on the east side. This was probably placed there to support the sundial. It is inscribed '1732 John Stanfoord, Lancelott James, Church Wardens'.

Weston Beggard. 149. 583/412
South of the church, dedicated to St John the Baptist, stands the base of a churchyard cross on three square steps. On these rest a square to octagonal socket-stone with hump corner stops and a niche with a round head. Following the destruction of the shaft with its head, it was turned into a sundial.

Whitchurch. 162. 549/176
Set just in front of the porch of St Dubricius' Church in this quiet spot on the banks of the River Wye are the remains of an ancient churchyard cross showing signs of a mixture of styles and ages. Its is believed to date from 1698. It stands on four circular steps on which rests a circular socket-stone reduced in diameter about halfway up by a bevel. This contains a projecting niche with a triangular hood, which covers the height of the stone. From this rises a square to octagonal shaft ornamented by dogtooth marks to a moulded cap and a Trinity cross of the gable-finial type. Both the shaft and the head are a later restoration.

Wilton. 162. 589/242
Watkins says that 100 yards or so below the bridge crossing the River Wye into Ross there was a Ferry Cross in a garden marking an old ferry crossing, but we were unable to find this. Situated half way across the bridge leading to Ross-on-Wye there is a substantial sundial standing on a square base. This continues in typical sundial shape before forming a square stone into which is set a gnomon and topped by a ball.

Winforton. 148. 299/469

A narrow track leads to the old church, now also in use as a community centre. In the centre of this track, where it leaves the main road, are the remains of a wayside cross, where, we were told, tithes were collected in the past. Watkins describes this as having the lowest of a tier of octagonal steps, saying the octagonal socket-stone is much worn. He wonders if this could have been put to some other use since the bottom is bevelled and the socket hole much enlarged. Today, all that remains is a ring of flat-topped stones. In the centre is a flat, apparently octagonal step on which rests an octagonal socket-stone still bearing its enlarged hole, into which it appears plants have been inserted. However when we saw it in early spring 2009 this socket-stone was not central to its step and we were told it had recently been knocked some way down the track by a lorry or truck. This appears to be a regular occurrence since we were also told that on previous occasions those responsible for Welsh Ancient Monuments (this village is very close to Offa's Dyke) have been called out and have replaced it on its original spot.

Withington. 149. 565/435

To the south of the nave of St Peter's Church are the remains of a cross mounted on three octagonal steps dating from around 1400, topped by a modern shaft and head. On this rests a plain octagonal socket-stone bearing a roughly cut niche with a crude ogee head. Letters incised into this can be read in part, telling us that the shaft and the head was made new in a restoration undertaken by 'R. Powell, M.A. the Rector, J.P. Appleby, and C.Child', churchwardens in 1897, to commemorate the sixtieth anniversary of Queen Victoria's coronation.

All that remains of the cross at Winforton, Hereford.

Woolhope. 149. 611/358

To the south of the nave, a square to octagonal socket-stone with pyramid stops rests on three square steps. The cross was restored in 1897 when a trefoil-headed brass plate was let into the west side of the stone recording this, which may cover a niche. The square to octagonal shaft has elaborate floral steps, and a capital and head of the nineteenth century.

Wormsley. 149. 427/478

Set on the top of a hill, with sheep and lambs keeping the churchyard grass in good condition, is the little church of St Mary the Virgin, another cared for by the Churches Conservation Trust. It has a twelfth-century font and reconstructed pulpit and lectern using Jacobean carved panels. Not far from the south porch is the base of a vanished stone cross of medieval date. Standing on two octagonal steps is a square socket-stone with worn corners and a hole where the shaft would have been. Also in the churchyard are some impressive tombstones.

Yarpole. 149. 470/649

Watkins mentions the step of an old cross that appeared to be the lowest tier of some steps, but there appear to be no remains now. This church (now in the process of being converted into a village centre) has a special treasure – that of a detached bell tower some 800 years old, one of seven detached towers to be found in Herefordshire. It has two storeys, the original wooden structure later being encased in stone. It also has a shingled roof and a spire. The great beams supporting this are a marvel of workmanship and well worth a visit.

Worcestershire

Alvechurch. 139. 026/724

Just outside the porch to the church stand the remains of a cross. Standing on two steps (the top with a bevelled edge) is a large socket-stone of two tiers. This bears a small portion of shaft.

Ashton-under-Hill. 150. 996/376

On the grass verge outside the entrance to the churchyard stands a tall high-cross situated on three steps. These support a solid bevelled-topped socket-stone with the remains of broaches at the angles. The square to octagonal shaft is in two stages, topped by a square cap to which the gnomon of a sundial has been added. When Pooley saw this in the 1860s he tells us the cap had been blown down and was at that time lying in a cottage garden close by. This did, however, make it possible to see that the east face held a sculptured blank escutcheon, probably at one time holding a coat of arms.

Astley. 138. 787/676

The church guide tells us that the remains of a churchyard cross to be found near the porch probably dates from the fourteenth century. The upper part is octagonal and the lower a square, the side of the upper part falling on the square having moulded steps. The upper face, we were told, has a square socket into which the shaft of the cross fitted, it

At Alvechurch, Worcestershire, two steps and a substantial base supports a very small part of a shaft.

having long since disappeared. However it was difficult to substantiate this claim since it was almost completely covered by ivy.

Belbroughton. 139. 919/768
In the churchyard, a modern octagonal shaft bears a carved head. It rests on four square steps and a square, bevelled-topped socket-stone. The church was closed on the several occasions we called.

Beoley. 139. 065/696
Beside the church porch stand the remains of a medieval cross, sheltered by a magnificent magnolia tree. Standing on three mossy square steps that supports a square socket-stone with bevelled corners is part of a worn shaft.

Berrow. 150. 793/342
There are the remains of an old churchyard cross, surrounded by flowers. The stocky shaft bearing a moulded top rests on a bevelled socket-stone, standing on three steps.

Broadwas. 150. 754/552
A short lane leads from the main Worcester road to Broadwas Church in the Teme valley. In the churchyard there is a restored cross standing on three steps and a square socket-stone bearing a niche from which part of its original shaft rises. The shaft is topped by a battlemented circle from which rises a Latin cross.

At Beoley, Worcestershire, the cross in the churchyard is sheltered by a magnificent magnolia tree and stands on mossy steps.

Castlemorton. 150. 794 372

In the churchyard of St Gregory, an old wooden cross stands on an original socket-stone. It is now firmly strapped with metal bands, the whole on two square steps of varying heights.

Chaddesley Corbett. 139. 891/735

Three steps and a bevelled square socket-stone support a square to octagonal shaft with a carved head. This was renovated in 1904 by the family of Lady Crease, of Sion House, in memory of Captain H.C. Oldnall, killed in South Africa during the Boer War. For many years the base of this ancient churchyard cross had been used to support a sundial pillar.

Childswickham. 150. 075/384

In the village at the foot of a lane leading to the church of St Mary is what is thought to be the remains of a preaching cross. Restored during the eighteenth century, it stands on a substantial lower step made up of three layers of stones and another narrower one. A two-tier socket-stone supports an octagonal shaft, capped and topped by an urn.

Clifton-upon-Teme. 149. 714/616

The church, with a modern shingled spire on a thirteenth-century tower, has in its churchyard an old cross. Standing on three steps, it has a bevelled square socket-stone with a round-headed niche from which rises a square to octagonal shaft topped by a wheel-head cross.

Cofton Hackett. 139. 012/753

Near the Lickey Hills stands an attractive small church with a pinnacled bellcot. Near to the porch are the worn remains of a churchyard cross, appearing rather unstable on two square steps. The socket-stone has incised into its four square sides a heraldic shield shape surrounded by roundels on each corner. A broken octagonal socket-stone, now minus any shaft, contains a stone that appears to be nothing to do with the original cross.

Cropthorne. 150. 000/451

In the churchyard, near to the road, is what appears to be a modern cross formed on traditional lines. Standing on two sturdy steps is a bevelled square socket-stone from which rises a square to octagonal shaft. Inside the church are the remains of an ancient Saxon cross, beautifully carved with birds and animals.

Eastham. 138. 656/687

Almost opposite the church porch (closed when we called) were what appeared to be the remains of a cross. There was a large octagonal set of separate stones on which was a pile of various sized stones. From these sprang the odd plant, looking to be self-seeded.

Eckington. 150. 922/415

Set on a triangle of grass in the centre of the village where four roads meet is a restored cross standing on two relatively small steps. The octagonal shaft is capped and topped by wheel-head cross beneath a pyramid.

Elmley Castle. 150. 982/415

At the entrance to the village, where a turning to the Combertons branches off, is sited a well worn old wayside cross. The shaft now stands in rather a dilapidated state, rising from

The wooden cross at Castle Morton, Worcestershire.

The cross at Castle Morton is a wooden one standing on its original socket stone.

a square socket-stone, its top bevelled to form an octagon. From this rises a worn shaft bearing incised markings and topped by a square two-tiered cap.

Elmley Lovett. 139. 865/697
Surrounded by trees in the churchyard here are the remains of an ancient churchyard cross that has been given a new top of a regulary cross with a central hole. It stands on three steps, a bevelled socket-stone with a square to octagonal tapering shaft.

Feckenham. 150. 009/616
Located in the churchyard of St John the Baptist and standing on four original steps and a three tiered socket-stone is a modern Latin cross.

Flyford Flavell. 150. 979/550
Near to the entrance gate of the churchyard stand the remains of a medieval cross. Supported on two square steps, a square socket-stone with bevelled corners is topped by an octagonal stone from which rises a modern tapering square shaft topped by a Latin cross. An old photograph shows us that an earlier shaft was much taller and topped by a wheel-head cross. This was restored following the First World War. It was later destroyed by a severe gale, until restored again as it appears today.

Frankley. 139. 999/804
This nineteenth-century church has in its churchyard a war memorial that stands on the foundations of the ancient churchyard cross. This stands on a square step on which is a square socket-stone. From this rises a heavy tapering shaft terminating in a wheel-head cross. The whole gives the appearance of being pretty modern but the church was closed and I've been unable to discover any further history about the cross.

Great Malvern. 150. 774/461
A postcard dated 1912 shows this cross to be mounted on three octagonal steps and a narrow bevelled square socket-stone. A niche appears towards the bottom of the octagonal

shaft and is topped by a lanternhead cross. The postcard image suggests that the cross has been recently restored.

Grimley. 150. 835/607

In the churchyard of an Italianate-looking church stand the remains of a medieval cross. On a square step, a square socket-stone with a bevelled top supports a capped shaft into which a sundial has been inserted.

Hampton. 150. 029/431

In the churchyard of St Andrew's Church, Hampton, near Evesham, are the remains of an old preaching cross. This stands on three steps and an octagonal deeply carved socket-stone supports a modern octagonal shaft capped and topped by a carved tabernacle head. The head is now very eroded.

Hampton Lovett. 150. 889/655

In the church of St Mary & All Saints stands a modern cross of medieval design erected in memory of Lady Pakington.

Hanbury. 150. 954/641

Where the foot of the roadway leading to the church meets the main road stands a small hill topped by the remains of an old cross. It stands on a square socket-stone with a bevel-led head from which rises a part-shaft. Since the village had a monastery in the past this could have been erected by local monks as a preaching cross.

Hanley Castle. 150. 839/419

Just to the entrance stand the remains of an old cross known locally as Hangman's Cross, due to the fact that it had earlier been found lying in a field on the Worcester Road a few yards before Hangman's Lane. When it was decided to erect a war memorial in 1922 this shaft was used, a new top in the old style being added. The cross stands on three steps, the central one bearing a heavy drip stone. A square socket-stone with a bevelled head has recently been added, from which rises an octagonal shaft topped by a sculpted head.

Standing by the Upton-upon-Severn to Worcester road there is an old cross. This is mounted on a small square step from which rises an octagonal tapering shaft with small niches near the capped top. The whole terminates in an attractive lantern-topped cross. An earlier postcard (probably dated around the 1940s) shows this as standing on a triangle of grass in the centre of a T-junction and surrounded by metal railings. The cross appears to be of modern construction.

Himbleton. 150. 946/587

Sheltered by a ring of spruce firs is a modern cross erected above the grave of Sir Douglas Galton.

Kempsey. 150. 858/490

In the churchyard are the remains of an old cross standing on two steps, a square base with a bevelled top and a sturdy tapering shaft topped by a small Latin cross.

Knighton-on-Teme. 138. 633/699

The cross in the churchyard of St Michael & All Angels is the remains of a medieval cross. Standing on three square steps, it has a worn octagonal socket-stone with a niche from which rises a part-shaft.

Mickleton. 151. 162/435

This village can be found on the Worcester/Warwickshire border and the church reached by steps or an ancient pathway. Standing on a window sill in the north aisle is what is thought to be the remains of a churchyard cross discovered last century during the digging of a grave.

Middle Littleton. 150. 081/470

Just to the right side of the porch of the church is a cross standing on three steps. From a square socket-stone rises an octagonal tapering shaft capped and topped by a fancy Latin cross.

Newland. 150. 804/474

Where the road turns towards Madresfield at the entrance to Malvern Link stands a large and imposing modern church. An old timber-framed church on the site was demolished in 1864, the original chancel being rebuilt to serve as a chapel in a burial ground. In the centre of the lawns in front of the building is a fine modern cross standing on two steps with overhang (the second bearing an inscription) and a square socket-stone also inscribed. The tall octagonal shaft is capped and topped with a pyramidal head and carved figures of a Madonna and a Calvary.

Ombersley, Worcestershire, has an ancient cross in the churchyard standing some way from the church itself. The earlier postcard shows the shaft to be very worn, so it has presumably had a new shaft fitted fairly recently.

Ombersley. 150. 843/635

In the large churchyard stands a cross on four tiered steps and a socket-stone in two parts, the upper one of which shows signs of being effective. From this rises what appears to be a very recent shaft, capped and topped by a square head beneath a pyramid top. A postcard dated around 1910 shows the shaft to be very worn, although the steps and head appear to be original.

Overbury. 150. 957/374

Here in the church of St Faith are two medieval consecration crosses that appear on either side of the chancel. Painted in the usual red-brown style, these are now slightly faded.

Pebworth. 150. 128/469

The remains of the cross here are badly worn. Supported in a square socket-stone with a bevelled top is a bevelled part-shaft.

Pershore. 150. 948/457

Situated in the grounds of the Abbey Church of Holy Cross stand the steps, base and shaft of a medieval cross.

Pirton. 150. 885/467

To the side of the church stands the part-shaft of a fourteenth-century preaching cross standing on a square base.

Queenhill. 150. 861/365

On a grassy patch by the entrance to the church of St Nicholas is a restored cross standing on three steps and with an octagonal socket-stone. The shaft is topped by a worked Latin cross beneath a pyramid head.

Ripple. 150. 875/378

Set in a gravelled triangle in the centre of the village are the remains of a tall cross thought to have been raised for the use of travellers on an ancient trackway.

Nearby, the remains of an ancient churchyard cross can be seen to the side of the path leading to the church. This cross consists of three steps and a bevelled socket-stone bearing a part-shaft.

Severnstoke. 150. 856/440

The churchyard cross here stands on a step comprised of smaller stones with bevelled tops beneath another square step. On this rests a square to octagonal socket-stone with bevelled corners and a pointed niche, from which rises a square to octagonal shaft topped by an iron crown. It is believed the cross was knocked down or removed during the Puritan era, when a group of Levellers resided in the village and nearby at Kempsey. The shaft was apparently discovered during Victorian times half buried in a spot just outside the churchyard boundary. It was re-erected on its present square stone base which is said to have been part of the old Upton Bridge, demolished in 1853. This could well be the case since prior to 1825 the Worcester to Tewkesbury road ran closer to the church than now. An early site plan shows a feature of some sort standing near the old entrance to the churchyard. Mr Bob Cross, who researched this cross, supports a locally held theory that the cross was transferred to this spot in the 1660s and used for a more secular and practical purpose. He suggests that the iron crown could well have been used for tethering horses and it is possible that after being rendered redundant by a new alignment to the turnpike road it fell or had been knocked over before being rediscovered years later.

Shelsley Beauchamp. 150. 731/628

In the churchyard of All Saints Church stands a sundial erected atop four steps and a bevelled socket-stone.

Shrawley. 150. 805/648

In the churchyard can be seen, standing on three steps, the remains of a churchyard cross. The top step is very worn. A sundial has been inserted into the two-tier bevelled square socket-stone.

South Littleton. 150. 075/462

By the south door of the church of St Michael stands the base of a fifteenth-century preaching cross, standing on two steps. From this rises a modern tapering octagonal shaft topped by a Latin cross.

Spetchley. 150. 895/540

Opposite the entrance to Spetchley Gardens (open to the public) is a small churchyard, the church itself being in the grounds of the house. At the top of a sloping pathway stand the

The cross at Shrawley, Worcestershire, has lost all signs of its shaft and in its place is a sundial.

remains of a village cross. Standing on three small octagonal steps and a short socket-stone, is an octagonal shaft topped by a modern lantern-head. Beneath are sculpted figures.

Stone. 139. 861/749

The old churchyard cross has a new octagonal shaft and battlemented wheel-head cross, but stands on its original three steps and bevelled socket-stone and now serves as a war memorial.

Strensham. 150. 911/405

It is known that in the past Strensham had a village cross, but this village is one that was swept away as a result of the Black Death. Following this a new village was established nearby. In the churchyard of the old church there is a large square stone that could be the base of a cross, but this is now almost completely covered by ivy and it is really impossible to tell. The church itself is well worth a visit. Among other treasures there is a fine gallery (probably part of the rood loft) holding a row of painted panels showing bishops and saints. Unfortunately the building, now in the care of the Redundant Churches Fund, was closed on our last visit, which admittedly was on a snowy day in January!

Suckley. 149. 721/516

All that remains of the old churchyard cross here are the three steps and a niched socket-stone, now collecting rainwater. Since the steps support a collection of rough greenery it forms an ideal spot for birds to rest, drink and bathe.

Tardebigge. 139. 995/691

In the churchyard here, flanked by the village school, are two treasures – a cross and an ancient yew tree. The yew's writhing and knarled golden trunk forms a mass of amazing and attractive shapes and designs. The cross stands on three mossy steps and square socket-stone carved with quatrefoils. From this rises a tapering octagonal shaft, now showing signs of age, topped by a Latin cross.

Tenbury Wells. 138. 594/683

Preserved in a glass case is a fragment of an ancient Saxon cross, carved with plait-work and serpents, and it is thought that a cavity in it may have held the relic of a saint.

Uckinghall. 150. 869/379

On the green in this tiny village stand the square base and sturdy part-shaft of a village cross, now very worn.

Upton Snodsbury. 150. 942/543

Just to the side of the church porch stand the remains of a cross. It is set on a square step and a tiered socket-stone from which rises a part-shaft.

Warndon. 150. 887/569

Mee mentions the shaft of a cross under yews but we could find nothing resembling even part of a medieval cross. However we did spy, near the entrance gate, a black metal cross

The original cross at Wyre Piddle,
Worcestershire, was moved to Pershore in 1844, a
copy being erected in its place.

bearing a plaque, dated 15 May 1980, stating it had been placed there to commemorate the
thirteenth centenary of the diocese of Worcester and dedicated to Christians past and present
who had worshipped there. Whether this was part of an older cross was difficult to tell.

Wick. 150. 962/452

An old churchyard cross is sited in a field next to the church of St Mary, almost opposite
Wick Manor House. It stands on three steps, the centre one of which is inscribed. A square,
bevelled top socket-stone supports a tapering octagonal shaft now bearing no head.

Wyre Piddle. 150. 967/475

The cross here is to be found at an off-set T-junction in the centre of the village.
An octagonal shaft topped by a stone cap and an iron cross stands on well-worn steps and
a sturdy base. Catherine M. Hammond, in her booklet *Wyre Piddle, the Passing Years* tells us
that the present cross is not the original since the remains of this were removed in March
1844. They had become 'decayed and dilapidated by course of time and were in great
danger of falling' as is reported in a memorandum to be found in an old chapel warden's
book, now at Worcester Record Office. A copy of the cross was therefore erected in its
place, to which was added a stone cap and an iron cross 'at the expense of a few voluntary
subscribers' under the direction of 'Reverend George St John, M.A., Rector of Warndon
and Curate of Wyre cum Throckmorton, Thomas Bomford, Churchwarden, and Pearse
St Audyn, Architect'. It seems unlikely the steps could have become as worn as they
appear during the last 150 years, but it is known that until the 1950s the cross was well
used by local lads as a meeting place. The original cross was then taken to Pershore where
it 'adorned grounds belonging to a private gentleman' situated next to the churchyard of
the Holy Cross (the abbey). This would have been in the grounds of Abbey House, the
Bedford family home. A bowling green now occupies the spot.

Bibliography

Bagley, J.J. & Putnam, G.P. (1960) *Life in Medieval England*. B.T. Batsford Ltd

Bord, Janet & Colin (1978) *The Secret Country*. Paladin Books

Bord, Janet & Colin (1974) *Mysterious Britain*. Granada Publishing

Dainton, Courtney (1957) *Clock Jacks & Bee Boles: A Dictionary of Country Sights*. Pheonix House

Diamond, Lucy (1944) *How the Gospel Came to Britain*. Oxford University Press

Ditchfield, P.H. (1889) *Our English Villages*. Methuen & Co.

Ditchfield, P.H. & Roe, F. (1994) *Vanishing England*. Studio Editions Ltd

Hammond, Catherine M. *Wyre Piddle: The Passing Years*

Hogg, Gary (1971) *Exploring Britain: The Shell Book of Britain*. John Baker

Lacey, Robert & Danziger, Danny (1999) *The Year 1000*. Little, Brown & Co.

Mee, Arthur (1950) *Gloucestershire – King's England Series*. Hodder & Stoughton

Mee, Arthur (1948) *Herefordshire – King's England Series*. Hodder & Stoughton

Mee, Arthur (1948) *Worcestershire – King's England Series*. Caxton Publishing Co. Ltd

Meller, Walter C. (1926) *Old Times*. T. Werner Laurie Ltd

Pooley, C. (1865) *Notes on Crosses of Gloustershire*. Longmans Green & Co.

Rimmer, Alred (1973) *Ancient Stone Crosses of England*. Garnstone Press

Taylor, Richard *How to Read a Church*. Ebury Publishing

Watkins, Alfred (1929) *Old Standing Crosses of Herefordshire*. Simpkin Marshall Ltd

Index